EMANCIPATION OF THE RUSSIAN SERFS

The emancipation of a serf. From a nineteenth-century print.
(The Bettmann Archive)

EMANCIPATION OF THE RUSSIAN SERFS

Edited by TERENCE EMMONS
Stanford University

HOLT, RINEHART AND WINSTON
New York · Chicago · San Francisco · Atlanta
Dallas · Montreal · Toronto · London · Sydney

Cover illustration: Punishment of serfs. From a
nineteenth-century print. *(Charles Phelps Cushing)*

Map on p. vi: Adapted from the map, "The Provincial
Divisions in European Russia, 1905," from *The Emergence
of Modern Russia, 1801-1917,* by Sergei Pushkarev. Copyright © 1963 by Holt, Rinehart and Winston, Inc. Used
by permission of Holt, Rinehart and Winston, Inc.

CONTENTS

THE PROVINCIAL DIVISIONS
IN EUROPEAN RUSSIA,
2nd Half of 19th Century

— Boundaries of major administrative regions

Black-soil provinces outside the Ukraine and New Russia

The provinces are named after their capital cities except
where indicated otherwise.

0   100   200   300   400   500
Miles

INTRODUCTION

Students familiar with the history of Western Europe are often surprised to learn that serfdom—the binding of the peasant to lord and land in servile status; an institution usually associated with the Middle Ages, a "natural" economy, and the absence of centralized political authority—existed in large areas of Eastern Europe until well into the nineteenth century, often in coexistence with extensively commercialized agriculture and highly centralized state systems. This geographical and chronological diversity constitutes a complex chapter in the historical evolution of Europe, but is beyond the focus of the present study. Here, we may simply note that the survival of serfdom in Eastern Europe into the nineteenth century variously involved such factors as relatively low density of population, relatively late development of urban life and nonagricultural economy, and the acquisition and the maintenance into modern times of political power by the landed nobility, either at the expense of or in cooperation with the central state authority—in a word, what is often referred to from a Western-centered viewpoint as Eastern Europe's historical "backwardness." [1]

Nowhere in Eastern Europe was the contrast with Western experience greater than in the immense Russian Empire, where the peasantry (constituting the vast majority of the population) lived in a state of servitude, bound either to noble landlords or to lands administered by state agencies, until the second half of the nineteenth century. Serfdom was a fundamental element of Russia's social and political structure until the day of its abolition; far from being a mere remnant of an ancient institution, it remained until the end a rigid system of personal dependency which very nearly equaled slavery, at least in so far as the status of the private landlord's serf was concerned. Accordingly, when abolition came, it was not a matter of awaiting the last gasp of a moribund body, but a deliberate act of state carried out in a burst of intense legislative activity. In promulgating this act, the Russian state undertook what was in many respects the most ambitious piece of social engineering in the modern history of Europe before the twentieth century.

Ambitious though it was, the emancipation of the Russian serfs did not solve that country's agrarian problems. Far from it. Mounting agrarian unrest in the late

[1] For a general interpretive introduction to the contrasting patterns in the history of European serfdom, see Jerome Blum, "The Rise of Serfdom in Eastern Europe," *American Historical Review*, vol. LXII, no. 4 (July, 1957).

nineteenth and early twentieth century led finally to the great peasant revolution which lay behind the dramatic political events of 1917. In the light of such events, scholars have looked to the emancipation as the point of departure for Russia's modern agrarian history and have drawn the most varied conclusions about its role in that history.

These remarks should provide some indication of the significance of the emancipation both in Russian history and in the history of Europe as a whole. In addition to being the most important event in the life of the Russian state between the reign of Peter the Great (1689-1725) and the twentieth-century revolutions, and an epochal event in the history of European serfdom, the emancipation is also a major historiographical battleground for conflicting theories about historical causation; about the relationship between broad developmental trends in society and willed actions by individuals; about relationships between state and society; about the nature of class conflicts, and many other questions. More than a few conflicting theories will be found in the selections that follow.

Russian scholarship on the emancipation of the serfs has been deeply affected by changing political and social conditions. Without dwelling on the details of this historiography, it may be said that the most obvious characteristic in its development has been its gradual expansion in a thematic sense. For the earliest, essentially contemporary, historians of the reform, the nearly exclusive object of interest and study was the preparation of the reform legislation and the political drama of the years in which that preparation occurred. As time passed, the reform came increasingly to be approached as an event in Russia's social and economic evolution, and the attention of historians accordingly followed a path outward from the politics of the reform's preparation to questions of its origins and long-range results. In the process, study of the emancipation as a distinct historical theme tended to become submerged in a mass of literature devoted to modern Russian social and economic development.

Although this historiographical trend cannot be neatly divided into two distinct stages separated by the Revolution of 1917, a qualitative distinction can be made between the predominant approach in pre-Revolutionary historiography and that of Soviet historiography, by and large. For pre-Revolutionary historians, the emancipation and the other reforms of the 1860s were part of a living tradition that made itself felt at every turn. To be sure, considerable attention was paid to social and economic aspects of the reform long before the Revolution, attention which was provoked by the enormous problems facing rural Russia in the late nineteenth and early twentieth century, but it was the emancipation as part of a *political* evolution—in which historians were themselves involved—that most excited their imaginations. The Revolution broke this tradition, and the sense of immediacy which had led to a view of the reform as part of an ongoing process—the liberalization of the autocratic regime—was lost. Yet, precisely because the Marxist view officially prevailed in the new Soviet regime, the emancipation has remained of crucial significance: Soviet historians regard the emancipation as a decisive moment in Russia's evolution from "feudalism" to "capitalism." In this outlook are revealed both virtues and shortcomings of Soviet historiography. On the one hand, the Revolution has afforded a perspective lacking to earlier historians and allowing the reform to be regarded as part of a completed process; and the general emphasis in Soviet historical scholarship on socioeconomic change has produced a number of important studies on the quantifiable aspects of such change as related to the reform. On the other hand, the emancipation, as a historiographical problem, has to some extent become a pawn in a neo-Scholastic concern with the proper interpretation and periodization of Russian history.

This historiographical experience will be reflected in the writings that follow. It should be pointed out, however, that the primary aim in selecting these has not been to represent fully the historiographical tradition, but rather to present important and influential discussions of the major problems surrounding the emancipation.

The first section contains two primarily descriptive pieces. One, by the American historian of rural Russia, Geroid T. Robinson, describes the institution of serfdom as it existed and affected the lives of the peasants in the last decades before its abolition. The other, by Soviet Academician N. M. Druzhinin, outlines the structure of the emancipation legislation.

An often-remarked characteristic of historical writing on the emancipation is the nearly universal acceptance there of the idea that the abolition of serfdom was ultimately necessitated by economic developments, an idea shared, in one way or another, by liberal and radical, Marxist and non-Marxist Russian scholars. But the specific nature of those developments and the manner in which the "necessity" of abolition was manifested have long been subjects of conflicting judgments. The second section is devoted to four major arguments on this theme. In the first selection, M. N. Pokrovskii, who was a Marxist historian with highly individual views on Russian historical development, emphasizes, in keeping with his general theory, the role of the penetration of the agrarian economy by commercial capitalism in bringing about the fall of serfdom. In reading Pokrovskii's argument, particular attention should be paid to his identification of the agents and beneficiaries of this development; to his reconstruction of the mechanics of the process; and to the kinds of evidence he musters in arguing his case.

The author of the second selection, the Russian economic historian P. B. Struve, draws an apparently diametrically opposite conclusion from that of Pokrovskii concerning the interests of the serf-owning gentry *(pomeshchiks)* in relation to emancipation. "Serfdom," he writes, "was abolished contrary to the interests of the *pomeshchik* class." Although Struve's work was published earlier than Pokrovskii's, his argument may be considered a reply to Pokrovskii, in so far as the latter's views on this question owed a great deal to the late-nineteenth-century writing on the economic origins of the emancipation, which was the direct target of Struve's polemic. In reading Struve's contribution, special attention should be given to the manner in which he disposes of the evidence cited by Pokrovskii and other contributors to this section in their affirmation of the economic decline of serfdom. Struve's alternative explanation for the fall of serfdom also demands careful scrutiny. What does he mean when he writes that "in human affairs there exists not only a necessity of the past and present, but also a necessity of the future"?

In the next selection a contemporary Soviet economic historian, N. A. Tsagolov, provides a critique of both Pokrovskii and Struve which might be called a standard post-Pokrovskian, or Leninist, analysis of the prereform development of Russia's agrarian order. Here the reader's main task would appear to lie in distinguishing between conclusions that follow persuasively from the evidence and those that depend on previously adopted theoretical postulates about the direction and processes of social development. In other words, does Tsagolov's rejection of the view that gentry landowners were becoming transformed into agrarian capitalists follow from the demonstrable evidence or from a dialectical view of historical change which dictates, among other things, that the "feudal" gentry class cannot be associated with capitalist development?

The final selection in the section is a translation of the conclusion to a book that appeared in 1967 on the Russian serf peasantry by I. D. Koval'chenko, a Soviet social and economic historian. His general theoretical position is essentially identical to that of Tsagolov. What is novel in his conclusion is the role he attributes to the peasant economy proper (as opposed to the demesne economy of the landlord) in agrarian economic development in general, and in the growth of commercial production in agriculture in particular, before 1861. His conclusions, which are based on extensive quantitative analysis in the body of his book, should be compared with the assessments of commercial activity in agriculture by the other authors.

The problem of establishing causal relationships between broad socioeconomic developments and specific historical events (such as revolutions) or deliberate human actions (such as reforms) is probably one of the most difficult and persistent problems with which historians have to deal. It comes squarely into play in writings on the preparation of the emancipation, the subject of the third section. Although several selections in this group offer what are in effect alternative explanations of the origins of the reform to those made in the first section, they all, unlike the arguments there, are directly concerned with the conscious motivations of the reform's planners and with the mechanics of its preparation. The selection by the British historian Hugh Seton-Watson performs the dual function of describing the most important individuals and institutions involved in preparation of the reform and of providing an assessment of that process in the tradition of liberal Russian scholarship.

Seton-Watson's account of the forces at work in the "politics of reform" may be compared with that of Soviet Academician M. V. Nechkina, author of the next selection. She offers a general critique of scholarship on the reform's preparation and attempts to provide a precise methodological solution to the problem of determining the relationship between socioeconomic developments and concrete political actions. It is the reader's task to judge the sufficiency of this solution, after considering the explicit theoretical foundations and the less explicit assumptions upon which it is based.

The selection by Alfred J. Rieber, an American historian of Russia, deals directly with the problem of the motivations of the reform's authors and those of Alexander II in particular. After subjecting the major interpretations of that problem to a critical review, Rieber offers an explanation in terms of the autocrat's recognition of the necessity—born of concern for Russia's international position—of reforming Russia's antiquated military structure. Although Russia's defeat in the Crimean War (1854–1856) has always been recognized as a decisive impetus to reform (beginning with testimony to its influence by contemporaries to the event), Rieber goes further than other scholars in attempting to identify the precise considerations involved.

Implicitly rejecting the primacy of the factors identified by Nechkina, another American historian of Russia, Alfred A. Skerpan, in the next selection, approaches the question of motivation, like Rieber, as a problem of *raison d'état*, but his emphasis is on the economic expectations of the state. Reviewing economic thought current in the early reign of Alexander II and in the preceding reign of Nicholas I, Skerpan suggests that the state's economic expectations were of fundamental importance in bringing about the decision to emancipate, while he argues elsewhere that these expectations were not realized because they were based on false theoretical premises. Among the questions that can properly be raised in connection with arguments of those who approach the reform in terms of *raison d'état* are the following: Do they succeed in identifying the motives they describe with the effective policy makers, as opposed to private or only tangentially involved individuals; and, if so, do they provide sufficient evidence to prove, or at least strongly indicate, that those motives were of decisive significance?

The historiographical theme, "the results of the emancipation" or, perhaps more exactly, "the significance of the emancipation for Russia's subsequent development," has elicited a great deal of controversy both within and without professional historical circles ever since the time of the great debate between Russian Populists and Marxists in the 1880s and 1890s about whether or not Russia was headed for "capitalism" on the Western model.[2] Three studies on this theme are presented in the final section. The first, by the prominent Italian historian and specialist on Russian Populism Franco Venturi, describes and analyzes the peasants' immediate response to the emancipation in the first two years after its proclamation. As Venturi shows, this was a period of extensive peasant disorders, particularly in the first months following the emancipation manifesto, and through analysis of the evidence on these disorders he attempts a comprehensive explanation both of the peasants' universally negative initial reaction to the manifesto and of the rapid decline of disorders after 1862.

[2] For a discussion of this debate, see A. P. Mendel, *Dilemmas of Progress in Tsarist Russia. Legal Marxism and Legal Populism* (Cambridge, Mass., 1961).

In the next selection, the foremost modern authority on the emancipation, P. A. Zaionchkovskii, sums up, from the point of view of contemporary Soviet historiography, the effect of the reform on Russia's general socioeconomic development. The emancipation is seen as having made an ambivalent contribution to capitalist development: On the one hand, it created certain necessary prerequisites for the capitalist development of the country, including primarily the formation of a reserve labor force; on the other, this kind of development was hampered by the preservation, in the reform, of "feudal survivals" in the form of labor rent, "extraeconomic constraints" on the peasants, etc. The result was capitalist development in a manner peculiar to Russia. In the opinion of Alexander Gerschenkron, a prominent American economic historian who has written extensively about Russian development, such an assessment is open to serious criticism. In a study of Russia's post-reform agrarian development which could not be included in the present collection, he argues that such an evaluation proceeds from "an implied view of a uniform process of industrialization repeating itself persistently from area to area . . ." which "is difficult of maintenance when confronted with broad empirical material." And he goes on to argue that it is "not the concept of prerequisites but the concept of substitutions for lacking 'prerequisites' that appears useful in understanding Russian economic development" after 1861. This concept, he concludes, renders problematical the effect on economic development of any such act as an agrarian reform.[3]

It is often assumed that the partial dispossession of the peasants in the reform, together with burdensome redemption payments and taxes, was chiefly responsible for the ills besetting Russian rural society and agriculture after 1861. The role of these factors, along with the economic implications of the retention of the peasant commune, is assessed by the agricultural economist G. P. Pavlovsky in the final selection. He argues that it was not the size of landholding and obligations or communal ownership, as such, so much as the type of land tenure and the level of technology, which kept the peasants in want; and not the agricultural system alone, but the state of the Russian economy as a whole, which kept rural Russia overcrowded and poor. Once again the reader is faced with the task of evaluating conflicting interpretations of the historical evidence.

[3] "Agrarian Policies and Industrialization, Russia, 1861–1914," *Cambridge Economic History of Europe,* vol. VI (New York, 1965), pp. 763, 764.

In the reprinted selections footnotes appearing in the original sources have in general been omitted unless they contribute to the argument or better understanding of the selection.

Professor of Russian history at Columbia University for many years, GEROID T. ROBINSON (b. 1892) has written what is very likely the only generally recognized classic of American scholarship on Russia. First published in 1932, his *Rural Russia under the Old Regime*, based on exhaustive research and travel in the Soviet Union in the mid-1920s, remains to this day the best English-language introduction to the social and economic history of pre-Revolutionary rural Russia.*

Geroid T. Robinson

The Peasants in the Last Decades of Serfdom

From the Golden Age of the Russian Nobility, with lace cuffs at court and iron-weighted flogging whips here and there in the villages, the proprietorial peasants came forth with the heavy tread of men in bondage, while most of their brothers on the State domains were also more severely burdened than before.[1] But it was not only in the external relations of the peasantry with the lords of the land that important changes had taken place; the internal life of the village had also been profoundly altered through a further development of collectivism. It has already been pointed out that in Old Muscovy, before the Time of Troubles, a number of neighboring households often held and cultivated strips of land in each of several adjacent fields, and at the same time made common use of pasture-lands and forests. For the conduct of their collective affairs, these groups of households held folk-meetings and elected elders who governed the land-relation of the members, and apportioned among them the tax-assessments laid against the commune as a unit. All this was important enough, but from the sixteenth century come the first records of a still more signifi-

[1] On the eve of Emancipation, approximately 22,000,000 peasant serfs lived in bondage to some 106,000 noble (gentry) landowners. A nearly equal number of peasants lived on lands administered by the Ministry of State Properties. Peasants of all categories numbered about 52,000,000 in a total population of the empire at that time of *ca.* 74,000,000.—Ed.

---

*Reprinted with permission of the Macmillan Company from *Rural Russia under the Old Regime, A History of the Landlord-Peasant World and a Prologue to the Peasant Revolution of 1917*, by Geroid T. Robinson. Copyright 1949 by Geroid T. Robinson, pp. 34–47, 48–51. Reference notes omitted.

cant manifestation of collectivism—the *re-distribution* of lands among the members of the commune.

Throughout the seventeenth, eighteenth, and nineteenth centuries, down to the Emancipation of the 'sixties, the practice of making periodically an equalizing redistribution of lands among neighboring peasants was spreading more and more widely through the country. It was in the old central-forest region that this practice first became general, both on the lands of the State and on those of the nobility. Nearer the frontiers, it was of a later growth, and among the peasants on the State lands of the North and of the nearer *step,* this kind of redistribution came to be widely practised only in the later decades of the eighteenth century or the first half of the nineteenth—and then in part at least as a result of official sponsorship. In the southern and southeastern areas, most recently colonized, redistribution was only beginning to appear on the eve of the Emancipation, and among the peasants of Lithuania, White Russia, and Little Russia or Ukraina, equalization by repartition was little known.

Some idea of the significance of the commune as a landholding and land-distributing body may be gained from the fact that in the general survey of Catherine's time, the lands used by the State peasants were laid off village by village, with no official attempt at a more minute division. In the actual conduct of a redistribution, the peasants were sometimes left quite to themselves, sometimes subjected to interference or control by officials on the State domains, or more especially by the landlords on those estates where the forced-labor system was maintained. The land was often apportioned by lot, sometimes in accordance with the number of workers of both sexes, sometimes in proportion to the number of males of all ages in each household (children included) who had been registered in the most recent census. Besides being a collective holder and partitioner of the peasant lands, the commune continued to be the collective bearer, and—in so far as the proprietors and the officials did not choose to interfere—the distributor, of assessments due to the landlords and to the State.

The periodic readjustment of landholdings, to keep pace with the procession of birth and death, maturity and decline, tended naturally toward the preservation of economic equality as between man and man within the commune. Further than this, through the employment of the communal authority in such fundamentally important matters as the apportionment of land and of taxes, there was provided for the peasant a continuous training in collective action, and this was naturally conducive to group activity in other directions. Sometimes, instead of distributing all the land, the village cultivated a certain area in common, and devoted the yield to a common purpose—perhaps to the relief of dependent members of the group, or to the payment of the tax-assessment. Sometimes the commune leased additional land from the State or from a neighboring proprietor, or even undertook to purchase land for the members' use, with the master's permission and in his name. Again it might build or lease a grist-mill, or make a common purchase of some such necessity as salt. Where the landlords maintained the system of *corvée* or forced labor, they often interfered in the affairs of the commune, but on the estates where dues were collected in kind or in money, and on the public domain, the peasants were left somewhat more to themselves. In the case of the State peasants, the village assemblies and their elective officers were given recognition in the laws of 1760 and 1761 and in a number of subsequent enactments, but in spite of all this, the local appointees of the government continued to interfere more or less as they pleased in the affairs of the State villages. Thus the commune was wide open to attack, whether proprietorial or official, from above; it acted only on sufferance, or—worse still—under duress; and yet the very existence of this collective apparatus with its collective functions, could not fail to be of profound importance in peasant life.

Somewhat less closely supervised than the proprietary peasants, the villagers on the State domains were also in a more favorable situation economically. Some of the State peasants were still attached to factories operated by the government, and were forced to work out their obligations there, but these formed in the nineteenth century only a minor group. In the 'forties, the new Ministry of State Property undertook an elaborate land-reform which was extended in the course of nearly twenty years' work to most of the *guberniias* or provinces of European Russia. By increasing the smaller allotments at the expense of the larger ones, and in some instances by the apportionment of additional State lands and by colonization, the cadastral commissions in some degree improved the situation of the poorer villagers on the State lands, but in 1866 the allotments of the State peasants still varied widely in size, from an average of about fifteen *desiatinas*[2] of non-waste land for each registered male in the northern *guberniias,* to one *desiatina* in the Little Russian *guberniia* of Poltava.

The amount of the dues assessed against the State peasants was proportioned to their total income, and therefore included a charge upon the proceeds of wage-work and of craft-industry as well as upon those of agriculture. However, these dues were distinctly more moderate than those which the private proprietors assessed against their serfs, and the more favorable situation of the State peasants, in respect to both the weight of their obligations and the size of their allotments, was destined to put its mark quite definitely upon the future of Russian agrarian history.

Geographically, the State domains and the lands of the private proprietors were intermingled, the former predominating toward the North, the latter in the South; and it was upon the serfs of the private estates that the age laid its heaviest burdens. The first half of the nineteenth century was marked by a number of regulatory measures which improved the position of these serfs, as far as the letter of the law was concerned, and seem in retrospect to indicate a reversal of the earlier official policy, and an advance toward emancipation; but in spite of all this, the peasants' allotments diminished, their obligations were increased, and the material weight of the servile system rested upon them even more heavily than before.

Before the opening of the century an important step had been taken toward defining the relation of the private peasantry with the soil: a regulation of 1798, applying to Little Russia[3] only, prohibited the sale of serfs apart from the land. In 1827 the subject was approached from the opposite side by a law of general application, which required the landlords to allot to their village serfs at least four and one-half *desiatinas* of land for each registered male, and prohibited any sale of land which would reduce below this minimum the allotments of the serfs remaining on the estate. Again, in 1841, nobles who were themselves landless were forbidden to buy serfs otherwise than with land. In the White Russian, Lithuanian and Little

---

[2] One *desiatina* = 2.7 acres.—Ed.

[3] The old-regime name for the Ukraine.—Ed.

Russian territories which had been secured through the partitions of Poland (nine *guberniias,* extending from Kovno and Vitebsk to Kiev and Podolsk), the earlier Polish-Lithuanian law had required the maintenance of "inventories" defining the allotments and the obligations of the serfs, and from the year 1844 onwards, the Russian authorities made some attempt to regulate the preparation and observance of these schedules. These various laws and regulations appeared to attribute to the peasant a right to the use of the soil—even to a certain minimum acreage; but side by side with this right, if there were such, there existed until 1858 another which constituted its negation—the right of the landlord to convert the serf, who normally supported himself by his own part-time labor on his own allotment, into a wholly dependent landless man, employed in continuous compulsory service about the manor-house or in the fields cultivated wholly for the provisioning and profit of that establishment. The great majority of the peasants were not subjected to this conversion; but even so, the laws which appeared to recognize their land-right remained almost entirely without effect, for the reason that there was no proper supervision to secure the observance of the inventory-schedules, and no serious attempt to enforce the all-important laws of 1827 and 1841. These measures may have prepared the way for those reformers who later maintained that when the serf was emancipated, he should receive a part of the land which he had previously occupied and cultivated; but the immediate effect in guaranteeing the serf a sufficient allotment was practically nil.

Actually the landlords cultivated directly an increasing proportion of the area of their estates, while the proportion allotted to the serfs for their own self-support declined. Partly on this account, and partly because of the growth (up to 1835) of the servile population, the mean area of the serf-allotments was diminished. The data on this subject are fragmentary in the extreme, but they seem to indicate a very considerable shrinkage in the size of the allotments. In most of the non-black-soil *guberniias,* the average plot would no more than suffice for the provisioning of the peasant family, and in a number of black-soil *guberniias,* the situation was still more desperate. Where, then, was the serf to find the means of meeting his obligations to the landlord and to the State?

Partly from choice and in part from bitterest necessity, many of the serfs not only cultivated their narrowing acres, but employed other means of supporting themselves and meeting their heavy dues; and like the private serfs, the peasants on the State domains also had their supplementary occupations. In the central-forest region, great numbers of villagers were engaged in part-time handicraft production, not simply to meet their household needs, but for exchange with their neighbors, and increasingly—with the development of the "domestic system"—for the account of merchants who disposed of the products in a widening market. With the permission of their stewards or owners, many thousands of the peasants of this same region left their villages for at least a part of the year to engage in wage-work or in trade in the towns. In the *step,* the peasants' chief source of supplementary income was not craft-production, urban wage-work, or trade, but agricultural work-for-wages on some nearby estate, or even at the end of a long seasonal pilgrimage into the labor-short *guberniias* toward the frontier.

Out of their earnings from such sources as these, or by laboring without payment in the fields under manorial cultivation, the serfs discharged their obligations to the proprietors. Here, as in the matter of the allotments, there appeared something in the way of a regulatory legislation: in 1797 an Imperial manifesto stated, apparently more as a pious maxim than as a law, that three days' forced labor each week was enough to satisfy the landlord's needs. This declaration was later interpreted as a prohibition against greater demands upon the peasants, but there is ample evidence that this prohibition was not everywhere enforced. As far as dues in kind and money were concerned, there was no pretence at official regulation, except in the half-hearted attempt to systematize and enforce the inventories in the western and southwestern *guberniias*. The Code of 1857 declared that the proprietor might lay upon his serf every kind of labor, and demand of him any sort of payment in goods and in money, with only these two restrictions of importance: that the serf should not be required to work for his master on Sunday, or on certain holidays, or for more than three days per week, and that he should not be ruined by the master's exactions. Such was the law, but history is more concerned with the fact.

On the estates where the system of forced labor or *barshchina* was employed, the serfs, men and women, were usually required to work for the master three days each week, or so to arrange matters among themselves as to supply an equivalent amount of labor; but not infrequently the demand was still heavier, and sometimes the proprietor kept his people at work continuously during the harvest, leaving them to gather their own crops as best they could, at night, on holidays, or after the manorial fields had been cleared. In the majority of cases, the serfs were obliged to supply not only the labor but the implements and the animals for the cultivation of the master's fields. Where the serfs paid dues or *obrok*, instead of rendering *corvée*, the assessments were substantially in-

creased between the last years of the eighteenth century and the Emancipation. Nevertheless the position of the *obrok* serfs was still very much to be preferred to that of those on *barshchina*, chiefly for the reason that, in the nature of things, the former were left much more to their own devices.

Toward the time of the Emancipation, the private serfs on *barshchina* out-numbered those on *obrok* by more than two to one in the forty-one *guberniias* for which data are available. The two systems were not everywhere mutually exclusive, however; and as the century advanced, the proportion of peasants who rendered both dues and services materially increased. In general, it may be said that the *obrok* system predominated in most of the *guberniias* from Moscow northward. Largely for the reason that the natural conditions here were not particularly favorable to agriculture, the proprietors of this region, instead of employing serf-labor extensively in manorial farming, preferred to lay on assessments which rested in considerable part upon the nonagricultural earnings of the villagers. Farther south, the landlords usually found it more profitable to employ their serfs in the plowing and reaping of the manorial fields.

The burdens of the servile system, heavy as they were, did not rest equally upon all the peasants of the private estates, or reduce them all to one common level of misery. Even in Great Russia, where the periodic redistribution of land by the communes worked toward the maintenance of economic equality, some serf families managed to accumulate goods and animals, and to draw other serfs into their hired service. In the western and southwestern *guberniias*, where the land-commune with its levelling tendencies was rarely found, the inequalities in landholding and in general economic condition were much more pronounced than in other quarters of the country. But although differentiation did exist, the well-found and prosperous peasant was to be discovered on the private estates only by exception; for most of the proprietary serfs, the half-century which preceded the Emancipation was a period not simply of static distress, but of increasing misery, sinking at intervals in many districts to the level of actual famine.

As long as the bound peasant had an allotment of land, and at least a part of his time free for its cultivation, and had also the responsibility for the housing, feeding and clothing of his family, he still enjoyed—whatever might be his obligations to the landlord and to the State—a certain measure of that autonomy which perhaps best serves to distinguish the daily life of the serf from that of the slave. However, as the new century advanced, a few Great Russian landlords, and a larger proportion of those of Little Russia, converted their estates almost literally into slave plantations, by merging the village fields with those of the manor and assuming at one and the same time the full direction of their peasants' labor and the full responsibility for their maintenance. Some of the landlords also carried on the manufacture of cloth, and other like industrial activities, and most of the serfs whom they put to this work were landless men; the number so employed, however, was not great, and toward the middle of the century it showed a tendency to decline. Large numbers of serfs were employed in the manorial apartments, kitchens, workshops, courtyards, and stables, and sometimes the proprietors even hired out their serfs to others, for work in factories or in the construction of roads and canals.

There is no means of determining with accuracy what proportion of the peasants had been affected by this debasement from an autonomous serfdom into a life of near-slavery. In general, the serfs who held al-

lotments, and were responsible for their own self-support, were officially registered as "bound peasants," while the greater part of the totally dependent landless serfs were registered as "courtyard people"; but in actual practice, many serfs who had held allotments were detached from the land and put to full-time work in the manorial fields, about the manor-house, or in factories, without any corresponding change in their official registration; and on the other hand, many who were carried on the registers as "courtyard people" had cattle, gardens, and separate dwellings, which gave them some degree of economic autonomy. Hence the statistical totals drawn from the registers do not give the true number of self-sufficient serfs on the one hand, and near-slaves on the other. However, since it may perhaps be supposed that these figures represent the situation with no greater inaccuracy at one time than at another, the very rapid increase in the proportion of registered "courtyard people" among the proprietorial serfs (an increase from 4.14 per cent in 1835 to 6.79 per cent in 1858) may probably be accepted as an indication of the growth of landless dependency. In 1858 the further registration of transfers of "bound peasants" into the status of "courtyard people," and likewise of transfers in the opposite direction, was prohibited; but during the seven years just preceding, the growth of registered dependency had been especially pronounced. If this evidence alone were considered, it might be said that not emancipation, but enslavement, was approaching.

In this control over the property and person of his serfs, the landlord was subject to limitations slight enough in theory, but of even less consequence in practice. Under a law of 1848 the serf might with the consent of his master acquire real property; but the master might call for evidence of ability to make the necessary payments, and then simply confiscate the peasant's savings. The proprietor was forbidden to reduce his serf to ruin, but on the other hand the serf was prohibited by law from bringing a civil suit against the master for his own protection, or from initiating a civil process against an outsider without the master's full consent. In sum, the serf had no property-rights which could be effectively defended against his master.

In respect to the person of the serf, the proprietor's control went far beyond the mere command of labor. He was still at full liberty to sell the serf with land, and although after 1822 it was unlawful to publish advertisements offering to dispose of serfs without land, such notices continued to appear, in the guise of offers to hire rather than to sell, and no attempt was made to stop the sales themselves. The separate sale of different members of a peasant family was forbidden by laws of 1833 and 1847, but there was hardly a minimum of enforcement. One enterprising landlord made a practice of purchasing orphaned serf-children, raising them on his estate, and selling the girls for marriage, and the young men to the landlords for use in meeting their quota of recruits, or to the State for settlement in Siberia. The proprietor might withhold the permission without which no marriage could be made on his estate; or he might—and frequently did—take the opposite course of pairing off his peasants, and marrying them whether they would or no. It was a common thing for the master to make what use he pleased of the girls and women of his household and his villages— sometimes in all the pomp and circumstance of a manorial seraglio; and such abuses were even less likely than others to be checked by official interference or the censure of neighboring proprietors.

Under the system of manorial justice, the proprietors had such wide powers to judge and to punish their serfs, that they could enforce compliance with almost any kind of extortionate demand. According to the Code of 1833, the proprietor was free to employ, for the maintenance of order and authority, any domestic means of correction which would not endanger life, or result in mutilation. Confinement and beating were common forms of punishment, and a devilish cunning had been employed in perfecting a whole arsenal of flogging instruments: rods, staffs, whips, bundles of leather thongs twisted with wire— sometimes, though certainly rarely, so zealously employed that the serf was beaten to death. The punishments permitted by the law of 1845 were still severe enough, since the proprietor might, for example, sentence a serf to four months' detention, or to forty blows with rods. The landlords might also dispose of offenders by sending them into the military service, or banishing them to Siberia; and in case of banishment, the wife and younger children were to accompany the husband, but boys over five years of age and girls over ten might be separated from the family and retained on the estate, if the proprietor so desired.

Instead of exercising the prerogative of manorial jurisdiction, the proprietor might at his option surrender the serf to public justice, but under the law of 1845 he was *compelled* to do this only where the offense, if against himself, his family, or another of his serfs, was a very serious one, or where the injured party was an outsider who preferred to carry his complaint to the public authorities.

As has been said, the proprietor was forbidden to ruin his serfs or to treat them with cruelty, and the law of 1845 provided that if these principles were violated, all the estates of the offending landlord should be taken under official guardianship. Enough has already been said to show that the law specifically sanctioned many practices which appear ruinous or cruel; but laxity in enforcement competed with laxity in the law itself, in contributing to peasant misery. There was really no adequate means for the discovery and punishment of the proprietors' offenses. The flow of information from its most natural source had been deliberately checked; the punishment provided for the peasant who complained against his master had been progressively ameliorated since the eighteenth century, but the law of 1845 still permitted as many as fifty blows with rods for this offense, and only in 1858 did the Minister of the Interior so far depart from the letter of the law as to make a distinction between just and unjust complaints, and to indicate that the latter might perhaps not necessitate the punishment of the complaining serf. But whatever the law might say, the peasants showered the officials with petitions, and although the petitioners were often severely dealt with, their complaints were received, as time went on, with a somewhat increased attention. The chief obstacle to the discovery of abuses, and to their elimination, once they were revealed, was that the enforcement of the law against a given proprietor depended so largely upon other members of the proprietorial class and upon officials under their political control or secretly in their pay. During the nineteenth century, official supervision made some advances against the arbitrary rule of the landlords, but these changes were so inconsiderable that, down to the era of the Emancipation, the proprietorial peasant remained without adequate means of defending such legal rights as now distinguished his bondage from full slavery. It is true that most of the proprietorial peasants were suffered to enjoy on their allotments a measure of the economic

autonomy which perhaps best differentiates serfdom from slavery; but this autonomy might be lost between dawn and dark, for even in the law the master was always free (at least until 1858) to detach the peasant from the soil, and convert him into a hand-to-mouth dependant of the manorial household.

Much has been said here of the trespasses of the landlords upon the narrow rights of the serfs, but there is no intention to imply in all this that the insecure frontiers of the law were never crossed in the opposite direction, by invasions of the serfs into the almost limitless domain of the manor-lord's prerogative. It will be shown hereafter that the opposition of the serfs to the law and practice of serfdom is one of the most characteristic and vital features of the manorial system; but first there remain to be considered certain other aspects of the internal life of the village.

Not only was the serf set apart from his master by a variety of economic, social, and political disabilities, but as the eighteenth century advanced, the cultural gap widened more and more. For the landlords, this was a century of education and Europeanization, carrying them farther and farther from the old Muscovy where the serfs and the peasants of the State still lived. Before the time of Peter the Great,[4] the villagers had been almost entirely innocent of formal education, and the grandiose projects of Peter and Catherine II[5] provided only a handful of villages with elementary schools. In 1804 another ambitious project was launched, and during the decades that intervened before the Emancipation, some progress was made in establishing official primary schools among the peasants. In addition to these official schools, there existed an indeterminable

---

[4] The first Russian emperor, who ruled from 1689 to 1725.—Ed.

[5] Ruled 1762–1796.—Ed.

number of unregistered primary schools, maintained sometimes by the peasants themselves and sometimes by the landlords. A beginning had thus been made, but the great mass of the serfs on the private estates and of the peasants on the State domains had hardly been touched by the cultural changes which since Peter's time had so deeply affected the nobles and the *bourgeoisie*.

Some few of the serfs, most often from among the "courtyard people," were, however, selected and trained for higher things. If the landlord maintained a school on the estate, it was likely to be devoted to the preparation of clerks and bailiffs, and perhaps to the preliminary education of other serfs who were destined to serve on the estate as barber-surgeons, surveyors, solicitors, or in some such technical capacity. Sometimes it pleased the proprietor to nurture the arts among his peasantry—to have some of them instructed in architecture, painting, poetry, music—to organize them into orchestras, ballets, opera troupes, or dramatic companies. To send a serf to a gymnasium or a university was forbidden in 1827, and again in 1843 (unless he was to be set free), but occasionally a proprietor even sent a favorite abroad to study—perhaps to become more cultivated, more European, than himself. Thus, in the matter of culture, a handful of serfs had crossed over into the masters' world—but was this likely to make them the more content with bondage? In the stories of talented and highly-trained serfs who sought liberation from their lot in flight, in drunkenness, even in suicide, there is some ground for thinking that this was hardly so.

But the tendency of the time was for the aristocracy to go their separate way, leaving the peasant mind to revolve within a pre-Petrine, even in part a pre-Christian, world. Pagan sprites and spirits still haunted the black forests and grey waters that lay between the log-built village and the pseudo-classical manor-house of the landlord, and in the peasant huts young men were nurtured and old men consoled by the repetition of folk-songs and folktales which often bore the mark of a dual pagan-Christian faith. It is true that on most of the estates, master and man still performed the same religious rites and listened to the same religious teachings, with Orthodoxy as a cultural tie between them; but sometimes even this bond had snapped, and the peasant had taken refuge in his own special "City of God."

Old Ritualism[6] continued to flourish among the peasants and the merchantry, and religious persecution provided the adherents with a special stimulus to fly to the frontiers, where they established settlements in the northern, southeastern and southwestern borderlands, and in Poland. That Old Ritualism was not purely a religious movement, is suggested by the fact that the Priestless branch proclaimed Peter the Great to be Antichrist come to earth, while the *Stranniki* or "Wanderers," an extremist group which arose among the Priestless late in the eighteenth century, were distinguished for a time by their denunciation of the Tsardom as a devil's rule, and their refusal to submit to official registration, to carry passports, or to pay taxes. Many of the Priestless, and the *Stranniki* in particular, refused to pray for the Tsar, and also repudiated the sacrament of matrimony, but the vast majority

---

[6] The conservative branch of Russian Orthodox Christianity which emerged from the great Church Schism during the reign of Tsar Alexis (1645–1676). The Old Ritualists, or Old Believers, refused to accept the revisions in ritual adopted by the church councils of that reign. Two main branches of the excommunicated Old Ritualists subsequently developed: the "Priestists," who perpetuated their own church hierarchy; and the more radical "Priestless" group which neglected continuation of the ecclesiastical order in anticipation of the Apocalypse.—Ed.

of these nevertheless formed family unions which were usually though not invariably permanent. The strong feeling of fraternity among the Old Ritualists or *Raskolniki,* and their custom of settling all disputes among themselves without recourse to any outside tribunal, gave their villages more than the usual degree of solidarity.

The propagation in the villages of a variety of evangelical and spiritualist teachings also helped to alienate the peasants from their masters. The *Dukhobortsy* or "Spirit-Wrestlers," and the *Molokane* or "Milk-Drinkers" (so-called because they drank milk on fast days, when it was forbidden to the Orthodox), first appeared in considerable numbers during the latter half of the eighteenth century. The *Khlysty* or "Flagellants," the *Skoptsy* or "Eunuchs," and a number of other sects were also propagated with some success. Both the *Dukhobortsy* and the *Molokane* condemned the institution of serfdom. Some of the former practised a thorough-going collectivism, with common flocks and herds, and "common granaries, from which each was supplied according to his needs," while a sub-sect of the *Molokane* undertook to establish ideal communes in the Caucasus and in Eastern Siberia. The *Dukhobortsy,* the *Molokane,* and the *Khlysty* did not forego conjugal union, but repudiated the sacrament of matrimony; the *Skoptsy* went far beyond this, in the practice of such a mutilation of both sexes as would make generation impossible. In the teachings and practices of the first two of these sects, an anti-Tsarist, or perhaps better, an anti-State tendency was clearly visible. A group of Dukhobortsy, imprisoned for their beliefs, prepared in 1791 a confession in which they said: "Verily the children of God have no need either of Tsars or of ruling powers or of any human laws whatever." Nor is this by any means a unique case of the repudiation of all temporal authority by members of this sect. Sometimes, too, they specifically refused to pay taxes or to pray for the Tsar, while the refusal to bear arms was general with them, and with the *Molokane* as well. In 1826 the *Molokane* would not pay their taxes, but a severe harrying by the government forced them to give in on this point. In a *Molokan* Confession of Faith printed abroad in 1865 it was declared that the members of this sect were obedient to the temporal power in all except spiritual matters, and that they regularly prayed for those in authority; nevertheless it is related that during the Crimean War, the *Molokane* had said that prayers ought to be offered for the defeat of the government which persecuted them, rather than for its success.

When peasant dissent meant at the least a kind of cultural separatism, and at the most a direct hostility to the manor-lord, the bishop, and the Tsar, even sometimes an all-inclusive repudiation of life through a refusal to propagate the species, it is not surprising that the government's attitude toward the dissenters was not exactly friendly. The earlier persecutions were considerably relaxed under Peter the Great, and still more in the time of Catherine II, but the accession of Nicholas I[7] brought a much more severe régime. In 1842 the government classified the dissidents in three groups: first, the *less pernicious* (those Old Ritualists who accepted priests), and second, the *pernicious* (the more moderate of the priestless Old Ritualists), both of which groups the officials were expected to hold in check, rather than to destroy; and third, the *most pernicious* group (the priestless Old Ritualists who repudiated marriage and refused to pray for the Tsar; and all such sects as the

---

[7] Reigned 1825–1855.—Ed.

Dukhobortsy and the *Molokane*) whom the government now hoped to hunt out and extirpate completely. The ill success of the official program is however indicated by the fact that about the middle of the century there were hardly less than a million sectarians and seven millions of Old Ritualists among the country's total population of some sixty-nine million persons . . .

In the expression of their discontent, the peasants not infrequently went far beyond the confines of song, prayer, and prophecy—sometimes to the length of a direct attack with torch and pitchfork. Where there was no major insubordination, the stubborn shirking and sabotage of the villagers sometimes so clogged the economy of an estate that the proprietor was obliged to sell it at a sacrifice, or to ask for an official guardianship. But the open forms of opposition were by no means lacking: among the peasants on the State domains, there were instances of disorder on a considerable scale, with furious repression in consequence, while with increasing frequency the proprietorial serfs carried their woes to the public authorities in hope of redress, or undertook by some forbidden act of their own to remedy their situation. For the last thirty-five years preceding the Emancipation of 1861, there have been tabulated 1186 instances of insubordination on the private estates—instances which in almost every case involve, not individuals, but groups of peasants, whole villages, even several estates with a number of neighboring villages. This tabulation is based chiefly upon the records of the Ministry of the Interior, and—at least up to 1854—the Ministry usually received reports only of the more serious disturbances; further than this, the table does not include arson, murder, or—in general—peasant flights; hence the figures by no means represent the full range of the

disturbances on the estates, and their principal value lies in the fact that they make possible a comparison of one period with another:

Instances of Insubordination on the Private Estates

Period	Total number	Average number per year
1826–29	88	22
1830–34	60	12
1835–39	78	16
1840–44	138	28
1845–49	207	41
1850–54	141	28
1855–61	474	68
Total	1186	

The official recording-apparatus was no doubt more sensitive during the period immediately preceding the Emancipation than during the earlier decades, but even when some allowance is made for this circumstance, there seems to be clear evidence of the presence in the villages of an increasingly active discontent.

As far as the very incomplete and one-sided records show, active insubordination was connected most often with a protest against the economic conditions of the servile life, and less frequently with an attempt to effect by one means or another a complete escape from the system of serfdom. Often it is not reported just what the disturbers did, but where the information is available, the most common manifestation is a refusal to work, or to pay dues, or to fulfil some other obligation to the proprietor. In general, these tables do not cover the more spectacular forms of attack, but it was not unheard of for the peasants to wrap a great manor-house in flames, or to devote the manor-lord to violent death in some one of its several forms. During the period 1835–1861, 30 bailiffs and 166 proprietors came thus to their end in the full climax of tragedy.

Instead of trying somehow to improve matters in the village, or taking a red vengeance upon the landlord, many of the serfs simply departed between the dark and the daylight, in search of a freer and better land. Sometimes a local crop-failure set them moving, but more often it was a rumor that in some distant place the bondsman could find freedom. Before the exodus from the *guberniia* of Vitebsk in 1847, it was reported there that the peasants of Great Russia had already been set free, and that all who desired freedom should hurry thither to receive it. Again, during the Crimean War, there was a rumor that freedom had been promised to everyone who would volunteer for the Russian military or naval service, and it was reported, too, that the English and French armies would liberate all the serfs who fled to them in the Crimea. Many of the serfs hoped for and expected some special dispensation from the Emperor; and once it was told about, that upon the top of a mountain at the Crimean isthmus, the Tsar of All the Russias was sitting in his golden cap, dispensing freedom to all who came promptly to his royal throne.

Of the number of individual flights, no serviceable estimate has ever been made; but sometimes the movement carried whole villages and groups of villages out along the road to the Promised Land. The flight from Vitebsk counted perhaps ten thousand persons; the movement at the time of the Crimean War affected ten *guberniias* in 1854, seven in 1855, and seven in 1857; from two *uezds* or counties in the *guberniia* of Ekaterinoslav, there were some nine thousand run-aways during the year 1856. And these were by no means the only mass-flights of the peasantry.

During the years 1826–1854, military detachments are known to have been employed in 228 different instances to restore order and authority in the villages, and to round up and return the fugitives. In the Vitebsk affair, one regiment, one battalion, and two additional companies were used, and during the Crimean War, with troops so badly needed elsewhere, there were employed to deal with the peasants in the *guberniia* of Kiev alone one full division of the army, one battalion of *chasseurs,* two companies of sappers, and sixteen squadrons of cavalry. Ordinarily the arrival of a detachment was enough to bring an immediate submission, but in rare instances there was a show of resistance, and in the *guberniia* of Kiev at the time of the great exodus thirty-seven peasants were killed, and fifty-seven wounded. The peasants were often brought before courts-martial—though this practice declined with the approach of the Emancipation—and flogging and exile were common forms of punishment; after the Vitebsk flights, some four thousand persons were beaten with rods.

Such, then, was the servile system, as the peasant saw it, from below. If we ask to what end it all existed—all the sweating at unpaid labor, all the flights, all the flogging and herding back to work again—the answer may best be sought for, not in the peasant's hut, but first of all in the manor-house of the proprietor.

An elder statesman of the Soviet historical profession, Academician N. M. DRUZHININ (b. 1886) has divided his long research career between studies of the Russian revolutionary movement and works on the social and economic history of nineteenth-century Russia. His huge two-volume study, *The State Peasants and the Reform of P. D. Kiselev* (1946, 1958; in Russian), is widely considered a classic of recent Soviet scholarship. A tireless contributor to collectively written general histories, Druzhinin wrote the article translated here for a recent text on nineteenth-century Russia.*

N. M. Druzhinin

The Emancipation Legislation

Composition of the legislative statutes of February 19, 1861 In addition to the "General Statute on Emancipated Peasants," sixteen legislative drafts, indissolubly connected with it, were ratified on February 19, 1861. These included the four general statutes concerning all *pomeshchik*[1] estates (on redemption, on household serfs, etc.); four statutes on the land organization of the peasants in the main regions of the empire (Great Russia, the Ukraine, Belorussia, and Lithuania); and eight special laws of a supplementary character (on the peasants of small-holding *pomeshchiks*, on mine and metallurgical workers, etc.). The fun-

damental questions resolved by the laws of February 19, 1861, were: the personal emancipation of the peasants; the allotments and obligations of the emancipated peasants; the redemption of land by the peasants; and the organization of peasant administration.

Personal emancipation of the peasants The enserfed peasants received personal liberty from the moment of the law's publication; that is, from March 5, 1861. From that day ended the right of the *pomeshchiks* to dispose of the peasants' persons—to sell, buy, give away, and mortgage them like things; to transfer them arbitrarily from place to place; to send them out to service or labor; to punish them, etc. The peasants immediately received personal and prop-

---

[1] *Pomeshchik:* owner of a *pomest'e,* a landed estate populated by serfs; *i.e.,* a gentry (noble) land and serf owner.—Ed.

---

*From *Istoriia SSSR. Tom II. 1861–1917. Period kapitalizma. Izdanie vtoroe, pererabotannoe* (*History of Russia. Volume II. 1861–1917. Period of Capitalism.* Second edition, revised). Moscow: Izdatel'stvo "Mysl'," 1965, pp. 23–33. Translated by Terence Emmons.

erty rights. Personal rights included freedom to marry without permission of the *pomeshchiks,* independent conclusion of contracts and obligations with private persons and the treasury, freedom to engage in trade and industry, independent conduct of legal affairs, both civil and criminal. In addition, the peasants as "free rural inhabitants" could henceforth participate voluntarily in organs of public self-government, enter other social orders (the urban classes, the merchantry, etc.), leave their place of residence, enroll in educational institutions and state service. The property rights that were extended to the emancipated peasants included the right to acquire movable and immovable property, to utilize freely and dispense with purchased land and to inherit property in accordance with local customs. The granting of personal and property rights to the former "subjects" of the *pomeshchiks* was the most progressive aspect of the 1861 statutes, in accordance with the requirements of bourgeois development.

However, the system of extraeconomic compulsion, as such, was not completely liquidated by the statutes of February 19, 1861. Despite their enlistment in the ranks of "free rural inhabitants," the peasants remained entangled in multifarious personal and property restrictions. Until the conclusion of redemption agreements with the *pomeshchiks,* the peasants were considered to be in a temporarily obligated state, and were obliged to submit to the seigneurial authority of the *pomeschik,* who could make a variety of demands on them through the village elders. During the first nine years after publication of the reform, the peasant did not have the right to refuse the land allotment and could not, therefore, leave the village community. And even after expiration of this term, release from the community was surrounded by numerous difficulties. Over the emancipated peasant's

head hung the mutual responsibility of all for punctual acquittal of cash and natural obligations: On the decision of the village community those in arrears could be forced to seek outside wages, placed under wardship, etc.; while those who paid punctually were obliged to make payments for the defaulters. All the peasants who had concluded redemption agreements and had become landed proprietors continued to constitute an unequal tax-bearing social order, obliged to furnish army recruits, to pay the capitation tax, and to submit to corporal punishment (from which members of the privileged orders—gentry, merchants, and clergy—were exempt).

Peasant allotments and obligations In determining the size of allotments and obligations, the law gave preference to voluntary agreements between the *pomeshchik* and the peasants but established one restriction—the existing allotment was not to be reduced below a designated norm. If such an agreement were not forthcoming, allotments and obligations were determined on the basis of the law. The statute on the peasants of the Great Russian, New Russian (i.e., southern Ukrainian), and Belorussian provinces, in which communal landholding prevailed, applied to the larger part of European Russia. This entire region was divided into three zones: the nonblack-soil, the black-soil, and the steppe; and each of these zones was further divided into several "localities," depending upon the level of soil fertility, population density, development of trade and crafts, etc. For each locality of the black-soil and nonblack-soil zones maximum and minimum allotment dimensions were determined (the minimum being one-third the maximum). If, before the reform, the peasants of a given estate held plots of land exceeding the dimensions of the *maximum* allotment, the surplus land was taken from them and given to the *pomeshchik.* If, on the contrary, the peasants' plots of land turned out to be smaller than the prescribed *minimum* allotment, the *pomeshchik* was obliged to give the peasants the quantity that was lacking or reduce peasant obligations proportionally. As a result of pressure from the serf owners, the allotment norms for each locality were set at such small dimensions that cutoffs of peasant lands in favor of the *pomeshchik* would everywhere be the general rule, while additions benefiting the peasants would be, on the contrary, a rare exception. Moreover, the *pomeshchik* had the right to demand reductions of peasant land if less than one-third the total quantity of land remained under his direct control. In the steppe zone, distinguished by an abundance of land and the prevalence of the fallow system of agriculture, one *dictated* allotment size was prescribed for each locality; but even here reduction of peasant plots was permitted if, as a result of the instituted allotment, the *pomeshchik* retained less than one-half the total quantity of land. Reduction was also made if the *pomeshchik*, in agreement with the peasants, turned over to them in property one-fourth of the maximum allotment without any redemption. Thus, mass expropriation of the allotment land used by the peasants under serfdom was predetermined in the territory of the Great Russian, Belorussian, and Southern Ukrainian lands.

The situation of the peasants was made even worse by the rules for constituting the allotment: According to the law the village communities were to receive only fertile lands, but it was also permissible to make allotments of salt marshes, with three *desiatinas* of salt marshes equal to one *desiatina* of the fertile lands due; nowhere did the peasants receive forest land, with the exception of the forested northern districts; and by demand of the *pomeshchik*, common and strip lands could be separated, peasant household plots could be transferred to new locations, and allotted lands could even be exchanged for others if the *pomeshchik* intended to build a mill, a factory, or the like. The allotment lands were considered communal and public: the household plots remained in the hereditary usage of the peasant families, while the field plots could be redistributed periodically, according to the decision of two-thirds of all heads of household in the village. By decision of the same two-thirds, and with the *pomeshchik's* agreement, the village community had the right to transfer from communal land usage to farmstead usage, splitting up all the land into hereditary plots once and for all.

Until transfer to redemption, the peasants were to acquit *barshchina* or *obrok* obligations for the allotted lands. Even here, however, certain substantial changes in the previous relations between the *pomeshchiks* and the peasants were introduced. The formerly collected dues in kind (fowl, eggs, mushrooms, etc.), as well as arbitrarily designated supplementary duties—watch duty, herding days, etc.—were abolished forever. The peasants of *barshchina* estates were granted the right to transfer from *barshchina* to *obrok* after two years from the day of the reform's promulgation, although under specific and rather burdensome conditions: announcement of their intention a year in advance and preliminary payment to the *pomeshchik* of half a year's *obrok*.

The dimensions of *obrok* were established in accordance with the level of development of crafts and trade, and fluctuated between 8 and 12 rubles per male serf for the maximum allotment. The size of cash *obrok* was lowered with reduction of the allotment; however, the change was not made proportionally, but on the basis of the so-called gradation of obligations; thus, for example, in the industrial nonblack-soil zone half the *obrok* fell on the first *desiatina* of the allotment, one-fourth on the second, and the last quarter was distributed evenly among the remaining *desiatinas*. In other regions the inequality in the distribution of the payment burden was somewhat less, but the intent of this ingenious system was the same everywhere: The *pomeshchiks* were assured receipt of their former income even in the event that the peasant took an incomplete allotment. It was also preliminarily calculated that *obrok* would be paid by the peasant not only from agricultural income, but from non agricultural income as well. The entire peasant commune was held responsible for acquittal of obligations according to the principle of mutual responsibility.

The fundamental rules pertaining to allotment of land and assessment of obligations which were adopted for the Great Russian, Belorussian, and Southern Ukrainian provinces were also extended to the remaining districts, albeit with certain local peculiarities. The statute on the peasants of left-bank Ukraine[2] and Sloboda Ukraine[3] sanctioned the existing farmstead-plot landownership and the extremely unequal distribution of land among the peasants. The land-allotment norms established here were even smaller than in the Great Russian provinces. The statute for right-bank Ukraine calculated allotments and obligations in accordance with the previously instituted inventories.[4] The statute on land arrangements for the peasants of Lithuania and part of Belorussia (where the struggle with the Polish national liberation movement was being waged) restricted somewhat the possibility of reductions of peasant land and lowered the

norms of existing obligations. Nevertheless, here, as in the entire territory of European Russia, the prescribed allotments were deliberately made insufficient for supplying the minimal subsistence needs of the peasant family.

The redemption operation A regulatory charter, officially confirmed and implemented in the course of the two years following promulgation of the reform, was drawn up for every estate. The mutual relations of the two parties fixed by the regulatory charters were regarded by the law as temporary, until conclusion of a redemption agreement on the allotted lands. Redemption was not declared obligatory, nor was a defined time limit for its institution stipulated, but following the 1861 reform it became much more difficult than earlier for the *pomeshchiks* to demand punctual fulfillment by the peasants of *barshchina* duties. This prompted the *pomeshchiks* to transfer the peasants to redemption. The transfer to redemption terminated the temporary-obligatory relations and thereby liquidated the system of feudal dependency.

The peasants lacked the ready cash needed for immediate redemption of the land from the *pomeshchik*. This was paid by the government in the form of a so-called redemption loan, which the peasants were to pay off in installments with interest. In calculating the redemption loan extended by the government for payment to the *pomeshchiks*, the law operated on the basis of the size of the cash *obrok* paid by the peasants for the land allotment that had been put at their disposal. It was intended that the *pomeshchik* should receive an amount of capital which would continue to give him a yearly income equal to the prescribed *obrok*. Therefore, the year's *obrok* was capitalized at 6 percent; *i.e.*, it was multiplied by 16⅔. In other words, an amount of capital was calculated which at 6 percent

---

[2] That is, the part of the Ukraine lying east of the Dnieper.—Ed.

[3] The region occupied by Kharkov province under the imperial administration.—Ed.

[4] Regulations on peasant land-usage and obligations introduced in that area by the government in the 1840s.—Ed.

annually would produce the sum of the former annual *obrok,* and, in addition, a supplementary sum designated for gradual liquidation of the loan and for administrative costs of the redemption operation. If the peasants redeemed the entire allotment used by them before the reform, the government issued to the *pomeshchik* a loan of four-fifths the computed capital sum; if the peasants acquired a reduced allotment in property, the loan constituted three-fourths of the capital sum. The difference between the computed capital sum and the redemption loan received by the *pomeshchik* from the state was to be made up to the *pomeshchik* by the peasants. If the transfer to redemption was made at the demand of the *pomeshchik,* the peasants did not make this additional payment. From the redemption loan paid to the *pomeshchik,* the government deducted the amount of the estate's debt to the [state] credit institutions, and the remainder was turned over to the *pomeshchiks* in credit securities (redemption certificates and bank notes).

The peasants were to liquidate the redemption loan in the course of forty-nine years through annual redemption payments that were collected by the government together with state, local, and communal taxes. The redemption payments were fixed at 6 percent of the redemption loan. From the moment of the state's confirmation of the redemption agreement, the peasants became owners of the redeemed allotments. Thus, with the assistance of the gentry's state, the *pomeshchiks* carried out an operation beneficial to themselves: in essence this was redemption by the peasants not of the land, which cost significantly less, but of feudal obligations calculated in exaggerated dimensions and capitalized at 6 percent; *i.e.,* at a high rate of interest.

Administration of the emancipated peasants
In place of the *pomeshchik* administering his peasant serfs, the Statute of 1861 established the peasant "commune" [*mir*], under the supervision of government organs. On the example of the administration of the state village, the peasants emancipated from servile dependence were grouped in village communities, and the village communities in larger units—*volosts.* A village community was constituted by the peasants living on the land of a given *pomeshchik;* the *volosts* incorporated adjacent village communities, with a [total] population of from 300 to 2000 male serfs. Each village community had a village assembly composed of the peasant heads of household and a village elder elected by the assembly for three years and serving as its executive. At the assembly village officials were elected and decisions on economic, organizational, and other questions of everyday life were made: on the distribution of land, apportionment and collection of obligations, family divisions and wardships, elections, etc. The elder convened the assembly and implemented its decisions. It was his responsibility to look after the communal economy, to assure punctual acquittal of obligations, and to fulfill police functions. For petty offenses the elder had the right to subject the peasants to fines (up to one ruble), compulsory labor, and arrest (up to two days).

The *volost* administration, placed above the village communities as a higher instance, was made up of the *volost* assembly, the *volost* elder, the *volost* administrative board, and the *volost* peasant court. The *volost* assembly, consisting of representatives elected from each ten households, rendered decisions on economic and public affairs concerning the *volost* as a whole (on recruitment obligations, organization of *volost* schools and *volost* reserve stores, etc.). The *volost* elder was elected at the *volost* assembly and, in addition to carrying out *volost* decisions, managing the *volost* economy, and supervising the village elders, he was involved in the police and administrative functions, which constituted the main sphere of his competence: he announced the laws and directives of the government, preserved general order, detained vagabonds, deserters, and criminals, etc. Together with the village elders, his assistants, and the tax collectors, he constituted the *volost* administrative board, a collegial organ that met from time to time for resolution of economic-administrative questions. The business correspondence of the *volost* board was conducted by a *volost* clerk. The *volost* elder had the right to impose penalties upon the peasants of the same dimensions as those imposed by the village elder. As for the *volost* court, it consisted of alternating judges chosen at the *volost* assembly. It dealt with the less significant property disputes among the peasants and the less important offenses committed by peasants of the *volost*. The *volost* court had the right to sentence guilty parties to compulsory labor (up to six days), fines (up to three rubles), arrest (up to seven days), and the birch rod (up to twenty strokes).

Above the organs of village and *volost* administration there was placed the authority of the peace mediator, who was elected from their midst by the local *pomeshchiks* of hereditary gentry status and was confirmed in office by the Senate upon presentation by the governor. The responsibilities of the peace mediator included: the settling of disputes between *pomeshchiks* and peasants; verification and confirmation of the regulatory charters; assistance in the conclusion of redemption agreements; and supervision over the actions of the elected peasant organs. Representing in his person the interest of the local landowners, this gentry-class agent was supposed to regulate the practical implementation of the reform with the assistance of the *volost* and village elders. According to

the law, the elected peasant officials were entirely subordinate to the peace mediator: he possessed the right to remove the elected peasant officials from their posts temporarily (until decision of the peace conference—as the gathering of all the peace mediators of a district was called), to reprove and reprimand the elders, to take them to court, subject them to fine and arrest, etc. It was possible to complain about the actions of the peace mediator to the district peace conference; that is, to the same local *pomeshchiks,* and about the decisions of the peace conference to the provincial office on peasant affairs, consisting of high provincial bureaucrats and representatives of the same gentry class. Thus, the elected peasant officials instituted by the Statute of 1861 were not agents of a genuine peasant self-government, nor were the village and *volost* assemblies, which were extremely limited in competence and subject to strong pressure from the obedient assistants of the peace mediator—the *volost* and village elders.

Emancipation of serf laborers and household serfs The household peasants and workers on estate enterprises were emancipated on special terms. They received personal liberty immediately but remained in a state of feudal dependence on their masters, the former for two years after promulgation of the statute; the latter until their transfer to redemption. Members of both groups retained only those pieces of land which had been given them under serfdom (household plots, haying parcels, field allotments). After two years the obligatory service of the household serfs was terminated, and if they had no land allotment (and such was the case for the overwhelming majority), they were obliged to register in the village or urban communities. The serf laborers were transferred to cash *obrok* (for the land they used) during the first two years, but could continue to work as hired laborers in the enterprise. The mine and metallurgical workers in private enterprises constituted a special category. The "masters" (those performing technical functions) were transferred to *obrok* upon confirmation of the regulatory charters; the "rural workers" (those who combined grain-growing with supplementary factory work) were gradually transferred to *obrok* in equal-size groups over a three-year period. The separation of the household serfs and the serf laborers from the land fills out the picture of the mass "clearing of the land for capitalism" which was instituted by the *pomeshchiks'* reform of 1861.

Laws on the appanage and state peasants Such was the basic content of the laws of February 19, 1861, on the abolition of serfdom on the *pomeshchiks'* estates. The main principles of the reform were extended, with certain peculiarities, to the appanage[5]

and state peasants. Personal freedom had already been presented to the appanage peasants by the ukase of 1858. By a special statute of 1863 they were transferred to obligatory redemption with preservation of their existing allotments, and in a few cases—where the allotment was extremely small—they received some additional land. With regard to the state peasants the Statute of 1866 was published, consolidating their existing allotments and granting them the permanent right of voluntary redemption of the land.[6] Both the appanage and state peasants were proclaimed proprietors and received the same administrative organization as the former *pomeshchiks'* serfs. Economically, the situation of the appanage and especially of the state peasants was better than that of the *pomeshchiks'* peasants: they received bigger allotments and made lower redemption payments for them.

[5] The peasants living under separate administration on the estates of the imperial family. They numbered about 2,000,000 persons.—Ed.

[6] In the case of the state peasants, however, the state provided no financing of redemption.—Ed.

The most famous name in Soviet historiography is that of M. N. POKROVSKII (1868–1932). Pokrovskii wrote the first general history of Russia from an explicitly Marxist viewpoint before World War I. After the Revolution, he combined writing and tireless publication of documents with the aggressive institutionalization, as a high government and academic official, of Soviet Marxist scholarship in history and other fields. Even before his death, however, Pokrovskii's own views on Russian historical development, in particular his view on the role of "commercial capitalism," began to be subjected to criticism, and for many years after his death he was condemned as an ideological heretic and his works were not republished until 1965. The following selection, taken from his general history, is a good example of both his style of writing and his application of the theory of commercial capitalism to modern Russian history.*

M. N. Pokrovskii

Gentry Capitalism, I

The thirty-year pause that separated the gentry movement of the 1850s from the epoch of secret societies was the political equivalent of those *economic* conditions in which the *pomeshchik* economy was placed from the 1820s through the 1840s. Caught in the vise of an agrarian crisis, the *pomeshchik* had things other than politics on his mind. To rebel against the authority which was the sole creditor of the entire gentry class would have been madness at a moment when only credit, and the cheapest possible credit, could save the *pomeshchik* economy from ruin. That same crisis made the old social forms precious. Gratuitous peasant labor, however inefficient it may have been, seemed the only possible foundation for large-scale agriculture. In economics as in politics, it was necessary to live according to the proverb: "Something is better than nothing." The agrarian crisis made the nobleman of Nicholas' reign at once a loyal subject and a defender of serfdom.

Under this apparently completely stagnant surface, however, there had been movement for some time. A vital stream was penetrating the serf economy from

*From M. N. Pokrovskii, *Russkaia istoriia s drevneishikh vremen. Tom 4. Izdanie piatoe (Russian History from Earliest Times.* Volume 4. Fifth edition). Leningrad: Gosudarstvennoe izdatel'stvo, 1924, pp. 45–55. Footnotes omitted. Translated by Terence Emmons.

that key area in which the entire economic life of Russia in the first half of Nicholas' reign was concentrated—the manufacturing industry. "The constant reduction in demand by foreign states for the primary product of our agriculture," says the author of a commentary *On the Situation of Workers in Russia* [1837] . . . "as well as closer study of the industrial resources of our own country were the main factors causing the *pomeshchiks* to try to direct a part of their people [that is, serfs] into industrial enterprises of various types. *This is the nearly universal trend of the present time.* Many such gentry establishments embellish the already significant industry of Russia in its most important branches." But the owner of the serf factory had long before come . . . to the "Manchesterian" idea of the superiority of "free" labor over serf labor. Through the intermediary of gentry employers the "Manchesterian" ideas were constantly to penetrate the gentry class as a whole. And there is no more well-founded or widely known fact than the *gentry Manchesterism* of the 1840s and 1850s. *The Barshchina economy is one of the least profitable forms of agricultural production,* so virtually all the "wide-awake" *pomeshchiks* of the end of Nicholas' reign affirmed in unison. They affirmed this with the same unanimity and persistence with which the contemporaries of Mikhail Shvitkov[1] had sung the praises of this same *barshchina* labor. "Look at *barshchina* labor," wrote the sober and circumspect Koshelev in the *Agricultural Gazette* in 1847. "The peasant arrives as late as possible, he has a look around as frequently and for as long as possible, and he works as little as possible—he hasn't a job to do, but a day to kill. He works three days [per week] for his

master and three days for himself as well. On his own days he cultivates more land, does all his household chores, and still has plenty of free time. Jobs for the master, especially those that cannot be set tasks, drive the zealous overseer either to despair or to rage. One punishes unwillingly, but resorts to this means as the only possible way of making some progress at the job. Now compare this work, even under a good foreman, with that of a peasant cooperative enterprise. There all is ablaze, materials cannot be readied quickly enough; they [workers in cooperative enterprises] will work for a shorter period than the *barshchina* peasant, will rest more than he, but will accomplish two or three times more. Why? Where there's a will there's a way." "One may boldly say," the Pskov *pomeshchik* Voinov wrote in 1852, "that *in well-run barshchina operations* three-fourths of the workers answer not only for themselves, but for others as well; that is, working time is increased by at least one-fourth." Toward the end of the 1850s similar arguments had become commonplace. The editing commissions[2] adhered to the proposition that hired labor is incomparably more productive than obligatory labor as if it were an axiom. Polemicizing with the editing commissions, Unkovskii based his calculations on what he considered to be the indisputable fact that after emancipation the *pomeshchik* would need only *two-thirds* as many hired laborers as *barshchina* peasants. Many asserted moreover, said Unkovskii, that the *pomeshchiks* could get by with only half as many; it was only to avoid error that he chose two-thirds. In the days of the editing commissions it was unnecessary to offer proof of such things, but such proof had

---

[1] A government official and writer on agriculture and political economy during the reign of Alexander I (1801–1825).—Ed.

[2] The government-appointed body responsible for drawing up the drafts of the emancipation legislation.—Ed.

been considered useful twenty years earlier, and it is worth introducing several statistical examples from the well-known memorandum by Zablotskii-Desiatovskii, written in 1840:

On the estate of *pomeshchik* A-v in Tula province, each household is given two *desiatinas* in every field, in addition to one *desiatina* of haying land and one *desiatina* of household plot; in all, eight *desiatinas*. Surplus land on the same estate is rented for 19, 20, and even 22 rubles per *desiatina*. Calculating even less—18 rubles— per *desiatina, each household costs the pomeshchik 144 rubles*. Consequently, an annual laborer and his wife will cost 288 rubles (since a household on this estate contributes three working days per week). In the same region:

A good laborer and his wife can be hired for	60 rubles
Their food costs	40 rubles
Interest, expenditures on horse, harness, implements and, finally, for housing these people, can be valued at no more than	70 rubles
Total	170 rubles

Consequently, 118 rubles less than a peasant household.

In Moscow district, "one prudent and perspicacious landowner" worked one part of his land with serfs and another with hired laborers. According to his calculations, translated into rye, it appeared that:

	Chetverts[3] of rye
A serf household cost the *pomeshchik*	21
A hired man and wife	20½
Income received by the *pomeshchik:*	
from the serf household	15½
from the hired man and wife	43

---

[3] A dry measure equal to 5.95 bushels.

Examples of bourgeois (merchant-owned) farms yielding 15 to 20 percent, and one even 57 percent, on invested capital are introduced in the same place. On the latter estate, for which detailed figures are given, more than nine *desiatinas* were plowed by each worker, whereas on the neighboring estate of Prince K-v, "the annual area of cultivation per laborer does not exceed five *desiatinas* with the most intensified *barshchina* (twice as much being cultivated for the *pomeshchik* as for the peasants)."

We will not discuss the accuracy of all these calculations. For our purposes what is important is that all the *pomeshchiks* of that time who were at all concerned about their farms and did not run them in routine fashion *thought* in this manner. We do not intend to criticize Zablotskii-Desiatovskii any more than we criticized Shvitkov. One fact is incontestable: bourgeois ideology made far-ranging conquests in the minds of owners of serf estates during the period of crisis. When the crisis began to abate toward the end of the 1840s, the Russian *pomeshchik* economy found itself confronted with competitive conditions completely unlike those of the days of Alexander I. Russia's place on the European grain market was being disputed by a number of *bourgeois* countries, both European and non-European, and competition with them led inevitably to the same conclusion: the necessity of making the transition to bourgeois relations in Russia itself. According to one contemporary author:

With the abolition in England of variable duties on foreign grain, competition was unbelievably intensified for Russian ports in general, and for the southern ports in particular, because even countries which had previously taken no part in the grain trade or had been little occupied with agriculture energetically took up this activity. Egypt restored the fertility of its soil and began efforts to market grain products. Export of grain from the Danubian Principalities became even more extensive, and in Rumelia the inhabitants took up agriculture in order to market products abroad. Even the North-American United States (that "even" sounds very nice to the reader of the early twentieth century) began to market their flour and corn in Western Europe at great profit. In such circumstances, the Russian heart involuntarily trembled with alarm over the future destiny of our ports, as well as about the very prosperity of predominantly agricultural southern and western Russia.

The Russian heart trembled for naught. Room was found for all on the grain market which once again opened up at the end of the 1840s, and termination of the agrarian crisis offered the most brilliant prospects precisely for southern and southwestern Russia. The horizon was truly darkened only much later, some thirty years afterward, when the Yankee, a foreigner who had accidentally wandered into the European grain exchange, began to rule autocratically over that exchange, dictating prices to Russian *pomeshchik* and Prussian *Junker* alike. But for the time being there was no need for concern about the immediate fate of Russian agriculture. Some alleviation of the crisis was felt as early as the late 1830s, as the table below will show.

Exports for 1838 were more than twice as high, by value, as exports for 1836, and almost twice as high as the average for the fifteen-year period. Grain prices were also

strengthened: "The price of wheat in St. Petersburg rose from 22 to 31 rubles per *chetvert;* in Riga from 22.50 rubles to 36 rubles; and in Odessa from 18 to 26 rubles per *chetvert.* The increase in the price of rye in St. Petersburg and Riga was also significant." But a real revolution in the grain market was brought about by the abolition of the corn laws in England and the famous crop failure of 1846 and 1847 in Western Europe. From the first of these events, the previously quoted author of the article on the grain trade in the southern Russian ports begins a new period in his history. He says:

The last period begins with the abolition, or alteration, of the variable grain duties in England, and later in Belgium, Holland and other states. *Trade in this product is becoming stabilized and can be more accurately calculated than for other articles of import.* This law not only protects the grain merchants, those from whom they purchase, and those to whom they sell, but even promotes expansion of exchange to unprecedented proportions.

The catastrophic significance of 1847 is shown by the table on page 30.

We see how ill-founded is the assertion, borrowed by certain recent scholars from Köppen, to the effect that the export of grain abroad played a very insignificant role, if any, in the grain trade of prereform Russia. Köppen himself neatly refuted his own most effective argument concerning the relatively negligible figure for exported grain (less than "a hundredth of the quantity required for the use of the empire it-

(in paper rubles)

Average [annual] value of Russian grain exports for 1824–1838 (according to Köppen)	Exports		
	1836	*1837*	*1838*
30,171,000	25,498,000	38,929,000	53,048,000

Price per *Chetvert* [in rubles]

Years	Wheat		Rye	
	In Odessa	In Tambov Province	In Odessa	In Tambov Province
1846	5.93	4.37	3.44	1.94
1847	8.14	4.42	4.17	4.42
1848	5.42	6.34	3.50	4.65
1849	5.74	4.66	3.56	1.96
1850	5.57	6.10	3.28	2.12

self"): by his calculations no more than ten million *chetverts* of all grains could be put on the market for Russia as a whole, while the average total harvest was about 180,000,000 [*chetverts*]. Nevertheless, "this remainder (a little more than 5 percent!) has, by means of the greater or lesser demand for it, a very strong influence on the price of grain in ordinary years." The foreign demand for grain which had been inflated at the end of the 1840s with catastrophic rapidity produced a veritable hurricane on the internal grain market. Even [the price of] such a peculiarly Russian grain as *rye* experienced a shake-up, rising in one year's time in Tambov (we have deliberately selected that backwater) two and one half times—taking the 1846 price as 100, we get 228 for the year 1847—and only gradually regaining the normal level. But in relation to rye, "disruptive factors" were undoubtedly involved: local good or bad harvests and internal consumption rates. The conjuncture of these "disruptive factors" with the influence of foreign demand led, for example, to the fact that in Petersburg rye prices for the entire period of the late 1840s only "held firm," showing no large fluctuations in either direction—about 6 silver rubles per *chetvert* (whereas the average price for the fifteen-year period of 1824–1838 had been 4.25 rubles). As far as *wheat*, primarily an export grain, is concerned, the fluctuations in its price caused by foreign countries are striking in their regularity. Odessa had only to raise the price, and Tambov, with exactly a one-year lag (the reader will not forget that at that time there was not even a hint of a railroad between Tambov and Odessa), reacted in the fullness of black-soil sentiment with prices raised still higher. However convincing Köppen's article may be, with its mass of precise and excellently selected figures, it remains purely a journalistic exercise—a reflection of that agitation for the construction of railroads which was conducted with such energy in the late 1830s and which shattered so pitifully against the deaf ears of the "aristocracy" surrounding Nicholas.

The influence of the 1847 catastrophe might have been transient had it not been merely the acute expression of a conjuncture which had been created by more enduring and persistent causes. Hence, although prices did fall somewhat after the first fever, the stimulus, once given, continued to act after the fever had passed. Calculating the prices of the 1820s as 100, we obtain the following progressive increases for the succeeding decades:

Decade	Wheat	Rye
1831–1840	113.84	115.70
1841–1850	138.06	141.26
1851–1860	174.14	190.13

These are the price fluctuations on the Berlin exchange, but, as they had in 1847, foreign countries continued to revolutionize our grain trade and, with it, our agriculture. Russian grain exports grew with fantastic rapidity. As we know, 1838 was an exceptionally good year for exports, although in that same year only a little over 20,000,000 *puds*[4] of wheat were exported, whereas in 1851 more than 22,000,000 *puds* were exported, in 1852 more than 40,000,000, and in 1853, 64,500,000! And just as in the sphere of prices, the movement abroad of quantities of grain provoked the movement of even greater quantities inside Russia. According to the data of the Central Administration of Communications, there were shipped on Russian waterways:

(thousands of *chetverts*)

	In 1851	In 1852	In 1853
Wheat	2,542	4,761	6,061
Rye	2,095	2,454	2,362

One cannot, of course, attach an absolute character to these figures. One and the same *chetvert* of rye or wheat was counted here several times: once in Saratov, for example; a second time in Rybinsk; and a third time on the Vyshnyi Volochek canal. But they do illustrate the *relationship* very well: in three years, *the turnover in grain increased two and one-half times.*

Russia finally emerged from its agrarian blind alley. Its providential destiny—to be the "granary of Europe"—which had been projected in the first quarter of the century but so considerably compromised subsequently, was no longer in any apparent

---

[4] One *pud* = 36 pounds.

doubt by the beginning of the third quarter [of the century]. Once again the serf estate began to produce for the market, and more energetically than ever before. It would be strange if this had not been reflected in *the internal structure of that estate,* and moreover in a very specific sense. *Large-scale agriculture based on serf labor was becoming increasingly bourgeois.* Capital was coming to play an ever greater role in it. Indebtedness of gentry landholding had already reached very significant proportions during the crisis. By 1833 about four million male serfs had been mortgaged to the various credit institutions of that time (the state loan bank, the guardianship councils, and the departments of public assistance). On these male serfs the treasury had loaned up to 950,000,000 paper rubles, or about 270,000,000 silver rubles. In this way the gentry acquired money, which had become a necessity for them, in view of the impossibility of acquiring it by the normal method of selling their grain on the market. Whoever has read Pushkin's correspondence will remember how frequently money is mentioned there. From it we can construct for ourselves a rather vivid picture of the extent of the demand for money among the contemporary higher gentry, to which Pushkin did not belong but with which he was compelled to keep pace. In one place he estimates his minimum annual expenditures at 30,000 rubles; in another, he speaks of 80,000 as the limit of his desires:—if he had that much he would be completely satisfied. There is mention of 125,000, but that is a dream, noted in connection with the income of a friend who had that much, although he was by no means one of the richest *pomeshchiks.* For these figures to be more comprehensible to us, we must translate the paper rubles of the 1830s into pre-[world] war [I] rubles; that is, multiply them by three-fourths, for that was the approximate relation between the paper ruble of that time and the metal ruble of the twentieth century. It turns out that ninety years ago 60,000 rubles was considered a barely decent income for a big Petersburg landowner. It goes without saying that Pushkin's estates, like those of all his relatives who are mentioned in the letters, were mortgaged, and we sometimes find the poet occupied with very prosaic cares concerning payment of interest to the pawnshop. But others besides substantial Petersburg gentlemen were debt ridden: that provincial neighbor concerning whom Pushkin teased his wife—"a man of 36, a retired officer or gentry official, pot-bellied and wearing a cap," in a word no aristocrat at all, "has 300 souls and goes to remortgage them in the event of a bad harvest." With the rise in grain prices in the late 1840s, the *pomeshchiks'* pecuniary difficulties should, it would seem, have ended; and if the gentry were borrowing exclusively for consumer purposes, as is usually thought, this should have been reflected in reduction of their indebtedness. But such was not the case; their indebtedness grew even more rapidly. From 270,000,000 (silver) rubles in 1833, it rose to 398,000,000 by 1855, and to 425,000,000 by 1859. By that year 65 percent of all male serfs belonging to the *pomeshchiks* were mortgaged, and there were provinces where an unmortgaged estate was a rarity. And these were, as a matter of fact, *black-soil* provinces, where the estate was progressively being transformed into a "grain factory" in response to the demands of the international market. First place on the list is occupied by the provinces of Kazan (with 84 percent of male serfs mortgaged), Orel, Penza, and Saratov (with 80 percent), Tula, Kaluga, Riazan, and Tambov (all with more than 70 percent). Their rank is broken by only one exception, but it confirms the rule: Above the last three provinces in indebtedness stood Perm, the old center of mining and metallurgy operating exclusively on the basis of serf labor. Credit was nearly exhausted in the black-soil region and in the Urals, but the need for capital, far from decreasing, was becoming more urgent with every year that passed. *Where to find the money for the further operation of their economy* had become a question of class self-preservation for the Russian gentry. There sprang up on this soil the first *practical* plan for peasant reform, arising not from juridical or moral considerations, but from purely economic calculations. This plan belonged to the man who was, without doubt, the most eminent representative of the old capitalism based on serfdom, the rich Riazan *pomeshchik* and tax farmer Koshelev. We saw a distant precursor of this plan in the Decembrist Iakushkin, but what he did or had planned to do piecemeal and on a small-scale was now being planned on a grand scale and was to be carried out through the exercise of state authority. The basic idea of this ingenious plan, which in the words of gentry and bourgeois publicists was given the handsome title of "emancipation of the peasants with land," was *to sell the peasants their freedom together with the allotments they had used under serfdom* and, having in this manner liquidated the old debt, to receive a new and equal amount of capital, no longer as a loan, but outright. According to Koshelev's calculations, which had actually exaggerated the extent of *pomeshchik* indebtedness, *pomeshchik* landholding, with its entire debt transferred to the emancipated peasants, could still produce as much as 450,000,000 silver rubles, while preserving the demesne intact and entirely free of all debts. We shall see that Koshelev's project differed little from the one that was in fact promulgated on February 19, and in so far as it did differ it was in the direction of greater modesty: The *pomeshchiks* managed to get more than their most calculating and enterprising representative had hoped for. True, the *pomeshchiks* lost in the bargain the right to the obligatory *barshchina* labor of the peasants, but that kind of labor was so little valued, and the superiority of the bourgeois method of farming was so apparent that—and this is a fact indisputably attested to from various quarters—*in the black-soil provinces an estate without peasants was valued no lower, and sometimes higher, than an estate with peasants.* It may be that in attributing no value to the latter the gentry of Manchesterian persuasion erred—this is what certain scholars would have us believe—although it must be said that such a widespread error would be an entirely exceptional event in history. But for one who is interested in economic history rather than economic theory, what is important is that *everybody thought in this manner* and acted in accordance with his conviction.

The road to emancipation of the peasants was now blocked only by the *inertia* of the most backward strata of the gentry. The strength of their inertia was sufficiently great to compel the introduction of a number of reservations into the reform which allowed the "emancipation" to be reduced to naught in some places, but it was nevertheless not great enough to halt the reform in principle. The reform could just as conceivably have occurred in 1854 as in 1861. If seven years of delay and four years of struggle were required before the progressive part of the gentry were able to realize their plan, the fault lay not with *society* but with the *government* (to use the then-current terminology). More properly speaking, it was the fault of that social group which had held power since 1825 and, having revealed no great political talents in the intervening years, had by the 1850s ended as a political force in complete bankruptcy.

Nearly all Russian students of the prereform serf economy agree that it entered a decline before 1861. The most significant rejection of this view, and one that has had considerable influence on Western scholarship, was made by P. B. STRUVE (1870–1944), brilliant Russian economist, historian, philosopher, and liberal politician, in a study first published in 1900. The following translation of the conclusion to Struve's controversial study summarizes both his critique of the majority position and his alternative interpretation.*

P. B. Struve

Gentry Capitalism, II

The ... development of the *pomeshchik* economy of central Russia encountered ... an obstacle in low prices. In general the serf economy was, of course, associated with a "rising" rather than a "falling" market, but the rise in prices progressed too irregularly and too slowly relative to the development of the economy. Regarding the interesting question of the economic significance of free labor in prereform Russia, important conclusions follow from the stated facts, which provide, in our opinion, a quite precise solution to this question. With the restricted nature of the market, reflected in low prices during good harvest years, it was necessary for agricultural proprietors that the monetary costs of production be *as low as possible*. Pay in kind for obligatory labor corresponded to this demand of the economy for the lowest possible monetary costs of production. The obligatory character of labor assured an absolutely low level of remuneration for labor; pay in kind for this labor in the form of land allotment reduced the sum total of monetary costs of production and by the same token reduced the total amount of produce which had to be thrown on a market already flooded in abundant harvest years.

We can acknowledge along with Zablotskii-Desiatovskii that prices on the Russian grain market (as everywhere else, by the way) were determined by the relation between supply and demand. However, due to the development of the *pomeshchik* econ-

*From P. B. Struve, *Krepostnoe khoziaistvo. Issledovaniia po ekonomicheskoi istorii Rossii v XVIII i XIX vv. (The Serf Economy. Studies in the Economic History of Russia in the XVIII and XIX Centuries.)* St. Petersburg: Izdanie M. i S. Sabashnikovykh, 1913, pp. 136–156. Footnotes omitted. Translated by Erica Brendel.

omy the supply of grain overtook the demand, and under these conditions the latter determined prices, contrary to the opinion of Zablotskii, who maintained that supply, based on grain production by serf labor, itself depressed prices. Of course, with the restricted nature of the market, the *barshchina* serf economy, which required no monetary compensation for one of the most important items of the costs of production—remuneration of the labor force—could, without undermining itself, go further in its concessions to demand than could a completely monetary economy. This constituted the economic strength, not the weakness, of the Russian prereform *pomeshchik* economy. Under the conditions described there could be no suggestion of the greater advantageousness of hired labor in comparison with obligatory labor, in so far as the mass of the agricultural work force was concerned.

Essentially, the theory of grain prices in the serf economy expounded by Zablotskii, if freed from the trappings of natural law, which are devoid of scientific meaning, can be reduced to the absurd proposition that low costs of production inevitably depress the price of a commodity beneath their own level. Such a theory requires no criticism. It was a bad and weak argument in favor of a good and powerful cause: the emancipation of the peasants.

The internal development of serf agriculture itself, therefore, was still far from reaching the point where liquidation of the economic content of serfdom would correspond to its interests. On the other hand, the development of the serf economy was undoubtedly headed for an agrarian crisis, the causes of which lay in the fact that the market was lagging behind production. We also know that the development of the serf economy, the growth of *barshchina* and its intensification, meant an increase in the exploitation of peasant labor, and how this provoked a reaction on the part of the enserfed peasants.

Thus, during the period of its greatest flourishing the serf economy was generating in its depths two major contradictions which cast a shadow over its future.

The knot of serfdom, as a purely legal phenomenon, was severed at once for all parts of Russia by the legislative act of February 19. This does not mean that the economic content of serfdom was identical at that moment in different parts of the country.

In the part of Russia under the *obrok* system, the serf economy, strictly speaking, did not exist. *Obrok* collected from the nonagricultural peasantry had been transformed into private taxation, a private tax on the income of small, and sometimes also large, producers. Its economic role, and, to an even greater extent, the economic role of *pomeshchik* authority in general, was exclusively negative here. This authority was exploited as a right, devoid of any economic content or justification.

Circumstances were different in the part of Russia under the *barshchina* system. *Barshchina* weighed on the individual peasant as a greater oppression than *obrok*, but this negative cultural significance of *barshchina* should not obscure for us its positive economic significance, the fact that, at the moment of its liquidation, the *barshchina* economy was the most productive organization of agricultural labor both objectively and in particular from the point of view of the recipients of surplus value. Possession of baptized property[1] could be a burden to the Russian *pomeshchiks* only in overpopulated localities, on the so-called small-holding estates. But we have no indications that *pomeshchiks* in

---

[1]That is, Christian serfs.—Ed.

these localities were actually so burdened by their peasants that they endeavored to get rid of them. Had this been so, we would have seen a mass liberation of peasants. This, however, did not occur. *Pomeshchiks* in land-scarce but fertile localities shifted from *barshchina* to *obrok*, resettled peasants on purchased lands, left a certain number of workers on their own plots of land, and finally converted them into household serfs; that is, paid them in monthly provisions; but nowhere do we see a conscious desire to get rid of serfs, even though their possession was bound up with a real obligation to support them in those cases when, for one or another valid reason, they were unable to provide for themselves.

Therefore, in the area under *obrok*, the organic development of productive forces was transforming *obrok* into an obligation more and more conspicuously laid on the person of the peasant and lacking any connection at all with the process of production. The receipt of *obrok* was a pleasant privilege in whose abrogation the *pomeshchiks* were not at all interested. *Pomeshchiks* exploiting peasants in the form of *barshchina* had no interest in the abolition of serfdom either; in the sphere of the *barshchina* economy, moreover, serfdom was still closely tied to the process of production, ensuring its most advantageous organization.

Thus, we come to the following conclusion, which is as yet only negative: *Serfdom was abolished contrary to the interests of the pomeshchik class.* The opposite opinion I consider absolutely lacking in any factual support and therefore incapable of withstanding criticism.

But how then, I will be asked, if not in terms of the interests of the ruling class, can we explain such a major reform? The development of humane ideas? But why did these ideas finally come into force in

the second half of the 1850s? This fact in itself still awaits explanation.

The lesson supplied by the Sevastopol defeat? I am not at all inclined to deny the enormous significance of that salutary lesson. But it was, after all, a historical accident, which in a certain sense might not have occurred; that is, the cause here came from without. It is enough to ask oneself, is it possible that if there had been no Sevastopol campaign the Russian peasants would not have been emancipated in the 1860s?—in order to eliminate that fact as a fundamental cause.

If I am told that the Crimean War was not an accidental phenomenon at all, that the war and its outcome were brought about by a quite definite course of our country's internal development, I reply: good, let us undertake an examination of that internal, and above all economic, development of the country. Can we not find in it explanations for the collapse of the serf order?

Before going on to an elucidation of that internal causal mechanism, which set unavoidably before the government the problem of a universal and simultaneous emancipation of all the peasants, I will investigate two questions.

It is quite clear that emancipation was not only in the interests of the peasants themselves but also corresponded completely to their desires. Does it not follow, therefore, that credit for emancipation should be given to the conscious and spontaneous strivings of the peasants themselves for freedom, to the peasant movements and disturbances? There is no doubt that this motive played a certain role in the decisions of the government, but the facts do not permit us to ascribe emancipation directly to this. It would be a ludicrous exaggeration to ascribe emancipation primarily to the peasantry itself and to its struggle against serfdom. This fact had rather the significance of a threat than of a really imminent danger.

Before going on to the positive significance of my negative conclusion, I will dispose of two possible objections. One of them is the well-known reference to the "devitalizing force" [*mertviashchaia sila*] of the serf condition. This concerns the decrease, attested to by a comparison between the eighth (1833–1836) and tenth (1857–1860) censuses, which occurred in the serf population during the period between the thirties and forties of the last century. I feel the need to dispose of the objection based on this fact all the more strongly since I myself, as far as I know, was the first in the recent literature to emphasize its significance for economic explanations of the collapse of the serf order. I cannot now personally maintain my previous opinion in its totality. The serf economy and the serf legal order themselves were, I am convinced, too complex an aggregate of economic relations to permit us to attribute poor population growth simply to the fact of peasant bondage. It is essential to dissect the phenomenon. . . . In fact, some parts of Russia, and in part *pomeshchik* territories, were overpopulated. But in such cases poor population growth arose primarily from that overpopulation, which could directly influence the death rate and the birth rate, increasing the death rate and decreasing the birth rate. But *pomeshchik* authority or serfdom could exercise a directly inhibiting influence only on the marriage rate. However, we have no facts which might indicate that *pomeshchiks* in Russia under serfdom, acting in their own interests, opposed imprudent marriages. They exerted pressure on the marriage rate only in so far as it was disadvantageous for them to lose workers as a result of marriages between their peasants and outsiders, and therefore they compelled their peasants to contract marriages among themselves. But this did not apply to overpopulated localities, since there was no reason to value the female working force there; on the contrary, it was advantageous to get rid of extra female mouths.

Briefly, if there was indeed overpopulation in agricultural Russia under serfdom, and if this retarded further population growth, decreasing the marriage and birth rates and increasing the death rate, then these facts were not connected with the fact of serfdom and the extent of *pomeshchik* authority that arose from it, but were determined by a factor of a more objective and fundamental nature: *the objective shortage—with the given distribution of land tenure and the given agricultural techniques—of food-producing land area.* Undoubtedly, this objective condition must have had an especially great effect on the *pomeshchik* peasants because these had less land than the state peasants, since resettlement of the latter entailed fewer difficulties than *pomeshchik* colonization, which was always associated with risk and expenditures for the *pomeshchik* and was therefore not as easy to accomplish.

However, the above-mentioned factor was rooted not in serfdom or in the serf economy, but rather in the distribution of land tenure, which has been preserved in its general outlines to this day, and in the objective conditions of production, which were independent of class relations. Briefly, even if it should be proven that the decrease in serf population is to be explained not only by transfers out of its ranks into other orders but also by a poorer natural population growth, the particular connection between this poor growth, and serfdom and the serf economy over a territory of any magnitude remains, in my opinion, not only unproven but in essence highly problematic.

I consider it necessary to draw attention to one more point that should be kept in mind in connection with this question. The percentage of serf population was very large precisely in those localities which were even then considered land-scarce and overpopulated, and also in those localities in which seasonal work was widespread. Both overpopulation and seasonal work could not help but decrease the percentage of serf population in relation to total population. The decline in the percentage of serfs which so amazed the abolitionists of the 1850s and 1860s was, therefore, a social inevitability, but a social inevitability *having no connection whatsoever with the serf order as such.*

These are the general foundations upon which I submit that the interpretation abolitionists of the 'fifties and 'sixties placed upon the fact of decrease in serf population and its poor growth relative to the natural rate of growth does not stand up to criticism from a scientific point of view. Once again we have before us *a poor argument in defense of a good cause.*

There is one more objection which must be disposed of. The opinion exists that at the moment of emancipation, the landed gentry, deeply in debt, was clearly headed for ruin. In support of this opinion, reference is made to the fact that in 1859, 39.5 percent of all estates and 65.5 percent of the entire serf population were mortgaged to the state credit institutions. But this fact by itself tells us nothing. Indebtedness becomes a heavy burden for landowners only when it is combined with a disadvantageous conjuncture, an unfavorable trend in income. The indebtedness of gentry land tenure in the last quarter of the nineteenth century, for example, was of such a nature, but prereform indebtedness was not.

In Russia under serfdom the opposite was the case: prices and incomes in general rose, and in part indebtedness itself testified to the flourishing state of the economy, in so far as debts were incurred in

the purchase of land, which brought in returns and rose in price, or in farming improvements. In any case, the average income of judiciously managed populated estates—to the extent that we can judge by indications throughout the literature—considerably exceeded payments on bank loans.

But the *pomeshchik* economy of the central black-soil region, ... suffered a peculiar crisis, and that crisis created conditions which—independently of all other factors of public and state life—had to lead to liquidation of the serf order. The serf economy of that region developed its productive forces on quite a large scale, basing itself on commodity production, while at the same time it had at its disposal a market too restricted and above all too unstable in its requirements and too disorganized.

The only realistic way out of this situation was an improvement in communications. This primary need of agriculture was pointed out in the 1830s and 1840s by agricultural proprietors themselves, as well as by the guardian of Russian agriculture, the Minister of State Properties, in his official report for the year 1846. There Count Kiselev wrote:

Our agriculture is still far from the condition in which it should be in Russia, an exclusively agricultural state; but it cannot be said that there is no development at all; of course, progress in this area cannot be measured in short spaces of time, but it is evident ...

Even so, it must be observed that complete success in the rational improvement of our agriculture can be assured only when labor and the capital used for it receive sufficient remuneration. Thus far our agricultural proprietors have not received that remuneration and complain of lack of demand and disadvantageousness of prices.

In 1846, both demand and good prices were to be found in the ports, but they had little influence toward an advantageous market for grain in the provinces distant from the ports, as a consequence of the vast distances impeding rapid and cheap delivery.

Therefore, the construction of new railroads undertaken according to the Imperial will of Your Majesty constitutes, in our present situation, an object of the greatest importance and any sacrifice made for such construction is justified by the sanctity of the aim itself: to increase the material well-being of the state entrusted to your charge, Most Gracious Sovereign, by Providence.

Thus, the very development of a commodity economy under serfdom in the agricultural center of Russia raised in turn the problem of railroad construction. One can say that if railroads had not already been invented in England, it would have been needful to invent them in Russia of the 1840s under the pressure of economic necessity.

An awareness of the necessity for improving communications was eloquently expressed in 1852 by Tegoborski in the following words:

Everything we have said on this subject confirms us in the belief that the future destiny and progress of our agriculture, in so far as they are in the realm of the possible, depend essentially and above all on the extension and perfection of our communications. In comparison with this great lever of national wealth, all other considerations which may influence, to a certain degree, the well-being of our agriculturalists, are only, in our opinion, of more or less secondary importance.

Thus the development of the serf economy in central Russia led it to the following contradiction: on the one hand, that development meant growth of the *barshchina* system; on the other, it created the need for a transformation of communications; that is, of market conditions, such as could not be reconciled, either with serfdom in its full extent, or even with any kind of intermediate form of peasant dependency.

The laying of railroads in itself constituted a revolution of greater economic significance than the mere proclamation of peasant freedom. It facilitated to a great extent the establishment of a money economy and revolutionized market conditions over a vast area. Any sensible person had to recognize that to build a network of railroads in the country and to maintain the serf economy in it was impossible. Nevertheless, the construction of railroads was, as I have attempted to show above, an urgent need of agriculture itself, and above all of *pomeshchik* agriculture. Nothing is more unhistorical than the view that does not see the organic economic link between railroad construction in the reign of Alexander II and the preceding development of our national economy, and, in particular, of agriculture.

Such are the economic foundations of the peasant reform. It is completely unnecessary to imagine that need for improved transport and only that served as a conscious motive for the peasant reform. I only wish to say that the development of the national economy itself created a situation which left no way out apart from liquidation of the serf system. The logic of the economic evolution of the *barshchina* center of Russia under serfdom in the 1840s and 1850s would in itself, without the shock of the Crimean campaign, without humane ideas, and aside from purely "state" considerations, have set this problem before the government. And there is a remarkable contradiction: The serf economy, approaching liquidation of the obligatory relations upon which it was based, at the same time, and once again by dint of the inner logic of its development, was constantly drawing the knot of *barshchina* exploitation tighter and tighter. Thus, the serf economy simultaneously moved further away from emancipation and drew nearer to it. The first tendency, retreat, was grasped and delineated with striking clarity in Samarin's note quoted above;[2] the second tendency, approach, was poorly recognized during the reign of Nicholas I, and indeed even in later times it was rather felt than recognized.

The two tendencies represented two sides of one and the same phenomenon. And if we consider the course of development of the serf order in Russia, we will perceive in it the subsequent peculiarity of Russian development.

Let us try for a moment to make a distinction between the concept of serfdom as the right to the entire person of the serf and the concept of serfdom as the right to obligatory agricultural labor. Serfdom in the first sense might have been abolished half a century earlier; even then it had become obsolete. It survived so long because historically it had become entangled and interwoven with the vital element, with the serf economy, which not even the most benevolent state power could have "abolished" before 1861.

Surviving until 1861 serfdom, by virtue of all the economic conditions of the time, also carried along with it the fundamental element of the serf economy: obligatory labor. However, if serfdom in the sense outlined above had been abolished earlier, that could not but have affected the fortunes of the serf economy as well. In that case—as has already been indicated in our literature, at least as a suggestion, by Mr.

Miliukov—a certain portion of peasants, not just household serfs, would already have been dispossessed of land before liquidation of obligatory labor. The tendency toward dispossession of the superfluous working force was undoubtedly characteristic in a substantial way of the *barshchina* serf economy of central Russia. It would undoubtedly have manifested itself still more intensely if serf relations had been regulated, if *the unrestricted authority of the pomeshchik over the person of the peasant had fallen away,* and these relations had been reduced exclusively to obligatory agricultural labor in return for land usage.

However that may be, in 1861 serfdom in its collapse could not help but carry away with it obligatory peasant labor as well.

But it was no accident that the *barshchina* serf economy was "liquidated" at a moment when it was flourishing. It was, as a result of this, liquidated in considerable measure only on paper. The new *pomeshchik* economy based on peasant implements is the prereform serf economy without obligatory labor. The real "swan song of the old productive process" turned out not to be a swan song at all, as the author of *Studies of our Postreform Public Economy* poetically described it; it was sung, and it is still being sung to this day throughout the entire expanse of our central black-soil region. The postreform agrarian order of the black-soil region, representing an extremely tenacious survival of the serf economy, can be inferred from the latter together with all the rest of its economic and social forms. That order is living and expressive proof of my conviction that the serf economy at the moment of liquidation of obligatory labor was still in a fully flourishing condition.

Thus, I submit, *the serf economy as such* had not matured economically before its abolition in 1861. Does this mean that the

---

2 ". . . According to Trubnikov's data, the population of the Imperial estates in Ardatov district [province of Nizhnii Novgorod] rose by 15 percent between the last two censuses, while that of the *pomeshchik* estates decreased. The mortality rate in the latter was especially increased among children. The estates, rather than undergoing subdivision, are growing in size, although slowly, and the number of small holdings is declining. There are, however, estates where the peasants have less than 3 meters [of land] per male—they are landless serf laborers." From a reform project by the gentry abolitionist Yu. F. Samarin (1819–1876).—Ed.

"stroke of the pen" which abolished serf-dom came too soon?

No, no, a thousand times no. An analysis of the serf order reveals to us the following remarkable fact: at a time when the serf economy still exhibited great vitality, significant portions of the serf legal order had completely fallen into decay and were threatening to collapse. It must not be forgotten that Russian serfdom was—as academician Storch had already shown with complete clarity, and as foreign observers constantly stressed—genuine slavery, or, in any case, was much closer to genuine slavery than was Western European hereditary subjection. It was, as Storch said in French, *esclavage* [slavery], and not *servage* [servitude]. The slave elements of the serf legal order had long ago become obsolete, and if the stroke of the pen destroyed them only in 1861, that was simply because history had tightly entangled and interwoven them with vital elements of the serf economy.

But the stroke of the pen did not come too soon even in relation to the serf economy itself. Internal social relations within agriculture had not prepared the way for abolition of unfree labor, but this does not mean that liquidation of the serf economy was not an *economic necessity*. In human affairs there exists not only a necessity of the past and present, but also a necessity of the future. The economic future was casting its gigantic shadow over the serf economy in the 1850s and 1860s and was making it *unsound,* despite its flourishing condition. Western European techniques were coming to Russia in all their forms—in the form of industrial techniques and in particular in the form of transportation and military techniques. Russia, crisscrossed by railroads, the laying of which also represented a complete revolution in economic conditions, could not have borne the bonds of unfree labor. The reform of February 19, in its economic meaning and content, therefore, did not so much sum up the past and present as it took into account the future; the very near future, to be sure, from which there was no escape by any route.

The conclusion I have reached states: it was not the internal development of the serf economy itself which led to its liquidation.

With some variations, the post-Pokrovskii period in Soviet historiography has witnessed the consolidation of a standard "Leninist" interpretation of the main processes and stages of modern Russian socioeconomic development. An able expositor of this interpretation is N. A. TSAGOLOV (b. 1904), a University of Moscow professor of political economy, who has written extensively on the history of Russian economic thought. The following excerpt from his work on the economic thought of the emancipation period conveniently contrasts this interpretation with that of Pokrovskii and of "bourgeois" (that is, pre-Revolutionary) scholarship.

N. A. Tsagolov

Systemic Contradictions

The fundamental error of the majority of scholars who investigated the disintegration of the serf economy is that they proceeded from the premise that a spontaneous development of the *pomeshchik* serf economy into a capitalist economy with the preservation of serfdom was possible. This profoundly erroneous thesis served as the methodological point of departure for a number of contradictory as well as similar conceptions.

M. N. Pokrovskii affirmed, for example, that the replacement of the serf form of economy was a matter of "purely economic calculation," that the *barshchina* economy was one of the most unprofitable forms of agricultural production, and that "large-scale agriculture based on serf labor became increasingly bourgeois" under the influence of rising grain prices. It was apparently an axiom for the author that large-scale agriculture based on serf labor could become bourgeois, and he argued only that it became *"increasingly* bourgeois." The author held that production *for the market* constituted in itself the transformation of feudal production into capitalist production.

That view is derived from the so-called "exchange conception" and the theory of "commercial capitalism" which M. N. Pokrovskii formally renounced, but whose methodological foundations he never overcame . . .

In order to demonstrate the inevitability of the transformation of the *pomeshchik*-serf

*From N. A. Tsagolov, *Ocherki russkoi ekonomicheskoi mysli perioda padeniia krepostnogo prava (Studies in Russian Economic Thought in the Period of the Fall of Serfdom)*. Moscow: Gosudarstvennoe izdatel'stvo politicheskoi literatury, 1956, pp. 38–51, 53–56. Footnotes omitted. Translated by Terence Emmons.

economy into a capitalist economy, M. N. Pokrovskii cited the data introduced in the well-known work of Zablotskii-Desiatovskii, "On the State of Serfdom in Russia," and also the article of A. Koshelev, "Where There's a Will There's a Way," which were supposed to confirm the greater profitability of hired labor in comparison with *barshchina*. But the simultaneous citation of these two articles, which argue different theses, in itself shows how superficial was the analysis of the question. If Zablotskii argued both the greater productivity and the greater profitability of hired labor for the *pomeshchik*, Koshelev, in the article "Where There's a Will There's a Way," argued only the greater productivity of hired labor. When, in fact, Koshelev elsewhere examined the question of the relative profitability of the two kinds of labor, he came to the following conclusion: "Of course, if one compares the [hired] laborer with the *barshchina* laborer one cannot but find him expensive."

P. Struve took the point of view that *barshchina* labor was more profitable than hired labor in the mid-nineteenth century.

Despite the diametrically opposed conclusions of M. N. Pokrovskii on the one hand and P. Struve on the other, they both approached the question of the relationship between the serf economy and the capitalist economy from false positions, by considering the automatic transformation of the former into the latter possible.

It is of course true that although the *pomeshchik* economy was not in fact transformed into a capitalist economy, capitalism was clearing a path for itself not only in industry but to a certain extent in agriculture as well. The developing capitalist elements in the countryside nourished bourgeois ideology and the bourgeois critique of serfdom. Granting this, however, it must be kept in mind that in so far as the developmental level of agrarian capitalism was incomparably lower than the developmental level of industrial capitalism, the character of the bourgeois critique of serfdom was determined primarily by the contradiction between the interests of capitalist industry and the existence of serfdom.

The internal contradictions of serfdom were no less profound in the agrarian sphere than in industry.

The fundamental relationship of feudal society in agriculture is manifested in feudal ground rent. The degeneration of feudal ground rent in nineteenth-century Russia was distinctly apparent, testifying to the crisis of the feudal-serf mode of production, to its transformation into a brake on the development of productive forces.

Two forms of feudal exploitation existed in nineteenth-century Russia: *barshchina* and *obrok*. In terms of numbers of serfs, the relative weight of *barshchina* was greater than the relative weight of the *obrok* form of feudal exploitation. But the relative weight of *obrok* had increased since the eighteenth century. Thus, the percentage of *obrok* peasants in twelve nonblack-soil provinces had risen from 55 to 58.9; and in seven black-soil provinces from 26.1 to 28.8.

Even these general figures show the enormous diversity in the relative weights of *barshchina* and *obrok*. If one takes the data for individual provinces, the differences in the relative weights of *barshchina* and *obrok* will become even more appreciable. Thus, for example, 12.5 percent of the serfs were on *barshchina* in Kostroma province in 1858, while in Tambov the percentage was 78. Moreover, the dynamics of the process in individual provinces show that the expansion of *obrok* was by no means universal. Thus, for example, the percentage of *barshchina* peasants in the nineteenth century, by comparison with the eighteenth century, had risen in Voronezh province from 36 to 55; in Orel from 66 to 72; and in Penza from 48 to 75. Thus, granting the general tendency toward increase in the percentage of *obrok* peasants, whole provinces are found with a clearly marked sharp increase in the percentage of *barshchina* peasants.

An increase in the percentage of *barshchina* peasants occurred in the black-soil provinces; that is, in the basic grain-producing regions of Central Russia. In New Russia,[1] the Ukraine, and the Don Army District, the percentage of *barshchina* peasants was everywhere above 95 and approached 100. Thus, the general increase of *obrok* peasants and the declining percentage of *barshchina* peasants conceal sharply contrasting trends in these percentages in individual provinces, a fact which shows that in characterizing the evolution of feudal rent it is impermissible to restrict oneself to establishing the increase in the total percentage of *obrok* peasants. The differences in the dynamics of the percentage of *obrok* and *barshchina* peasants conceal contrasting forms of disintegration and crisis in the serf economy in individual regions of Russia determined by differences in their economic conditions. This must be borne in mind above all in order to avoid the hasty conclusion that the nineteenth century is characterized by systematic growth in the *obrok* system of serf production in *agriculture*. In fact, there are grounds for drawing the opposite conclusion, if changes in the level of employment of *barshchina* labor are taken into consideration.

In the course of the first half of the nineteenth century, the *pomeshchiks* took enormous expanses of land away from the peasants. Thus, at the end of the eighteenth century the *pomeshchiks* held 18 percent of the land and the peasants 72 percent in

[1] The fertile steppe area immediately north of the Black Sea.—Ed.

the black-soil provinces. By the middle of the nineteenth century, the *pomeshchiks* of these provinces held 49 percent and the peasants 51 percent. In eight nonblack-soil provinces the percentage of land in *pomeshchik* hands rose from 14 to 25, and the percentage of land in peasant hands fell from 86 to 75. The increase in demesne, cultivated of course by serfs, signifies, in so far as there were no serious indications of technical progress in agricultural production, an increase in *the total quantity* of expended *surplus labor. The total quantity of barshchina labor expended in agriculture, far from declining, actually increased.* This hypothesis is confirmed by the increase in the number of *barshchina* days—a universally observed phenomenon in the nineteenth century. Thus, despite a decline in the over-all percentage of *barshchina* peasants, a growing share of agricultural production was carried out by *barshchina* methods.

On the one hand the percentage of *barshchina* peasants decreased, but on the other hand the percentage of *barshchina* labor applied to agricultural production increased. Such was the real, contradictory picture of the development of agriculture under serfdom. The growth in the relative weight of *obrok* peasants facilitated an increase in the mass of labor power placed on the labor market and played a positive role in the development of capitalist relations. This was not, however, the expression of a progressive tendency in the evolution of feudal ground rent; that is, a tendency toward isolation of feudal landed property from agricultural production . . .

Thus, the existence of both money rent and labor rent does not in the present case signify the coexistence in the Russian feudal-serf order of two economic systems which were sharply different in their methods of producing surplus product. In both cases rent appeared in the form of money, but in one case it came directly from the exploited producer in monetary form, while in the other case it was appropriated in the form of labor and was only subsequently the product of this labor transformed into money.

The tendency toward growth of the *obrok* system was characteristic primarily of the nonblack-soil provinces and reflected an ever-increasing effort on the part of the serf owners to gain control over surplus labor outside the sphere of agriculture.

As long as peasant industry retained the form of a domestic industry united with agriculture, appropriation by the feudal lord of the surplus product created by both agricultural and industrial labor could not have serious national-economic significance. The scale of industrial activity was relatively insignificant and the method of production was handicraft. But in the nineteenth century industrial activity began to be isolated [from agriculture], the scale of industry grew significantly, and techniques changed, evolving in the 1840s and 1850s toward machine production. Capitalist enterprises began to play the principal role in industry.

In the nineteenth century the relative, and later also the absolute, magnitude of industry based on serfdom declined. But this does not indicate a decline in the magnitude of surplus product created in industry and *appropriated* by the serf owners. There was a tendency toward decline in the magnitude of industrial surplus product *created* under the command of the serf owner, but to make up for it there was a noticeable tendency toward growth in the total quantity of surplus product produced under the command of the capitalist and appropriated by the serf owners.

The dimensions of industrial surplus product produced by capitalist methods significantly increased. The accumulation of capital became a necessary condition for the normal development of an industry

that had gone over to the capitalist system of productive relations. The intrusion of the feudal lord into this sphere of social production constituted a serious hindrance to its development. The growth of the *obrok* system in nineteenth-century Russia reflected the gradual transformation of money rent from a form of surplus product, produced in feudally organized agriculture and appropriated by the feudal lord, into a form of appropriation by the feudal lord of a surplus product produced in capitalistically organized industry.

The growth in the relative weight and numbers of *obrok* peasants, the growth in the size of *obrok* per unit of peasant labor, the geographical distribution of the overwhelming mass of *obrok* peasants, and, finally, the complete triumph of money *obrok* over payment in kind all this constitutes an expression of *the expansion of the sources of feudal rent*, their expansion beyond the bounds of agriculture and peasant domestic industry. The growth-dynamics of *obrok* show that the source of its increase could not have been agricultural labor alone. At the beginning of the eighteenth century, *obrok* went as high as 1 ruble per registered serf; in the middle of that century, 2 rubles; at the beginning of the nineteenth century, 5 rubles. By the mid-nineteenth century, *obrok* was as high as 20 to 24 rubles per household. It is true that simultaneously with the increase in *obrok* there occurred an increase in grain prices, but the increase in *obrok* significantly outdistanced the increase in grain prices . . . That *obrok* extended beyond the confines of agricultural surplus labor is evident from the differentiation in the size of *obrok* among the peasants of one and the same *pomeshchik*, and from the dimensions of *obrok*, which testify to the fact that these *obrok* obligations were being paid not by serfs who worked the land, but by serfs who themselves exploited others . . .

The parasitic character of *obrok,* as of any feudal rent, needs no proof. *Obrok* which extended beyond the confines of the feudal village became doubly parasitic. It was transformed into a brake on the development of those more progressive forms of social production which had already made their appearance; in this case, capitalist industry. *Obrok* was not a form of supplementary gain, and its limit was certainly not average profit. Arbitrarily established *obrok* (money rent) was itself the limit of profit. Here it was not profit that determined rent, but rather rent that determined the magnitude of profit.

Thus, in nineteenth-century Russia a growth both of *obrok* and of *barshchina* took place. Such an assertion is contradictory and absurd if *barshchina* and *obrok* in the nineteenth century are regarded as forms of feudal exploitation in the sphere of agriculture. But if the above-mentioned trends of change in the source of *obrok* are borne in mind, it will be clear that those two phenomena were in fact fully compatible . . .

As we saw above, the increase in the number of *obrok* serfs was accompanied by growth of the demesne and reduction of [peasant] allotments. Thus, neither the separation of landed property from agricultural production, nor the emancipation of the direct agricultural producer from "direct compulsion" (Marx) were taking place. On the contrary, all the signs of an expansion of the processes of separation of the direct producer from the land and the joining of agricultural production to feudal landed property were present. Here is the economic expression of the fact that the measure of the peasant's surplus labor was becoming progressively emancipated from the size of the allotment. Growth in the number of *obrok* peasants and in the size of *obrok* accompanied by the diminution of

the allotments is an illustration of that thesis.

The increase in *obrok* rates aggravated the contradictions between serfdom and the burgeoning capitalist industry, and the growth of *barshchina* became the point of departure for a crisis of the serf mode of production in agriculture. The increase in *barshchina* obligations in the nineteenth century, in contrast to preceding centuries, was bound up with the development of commercial agriculture in the *pomeshchik* economy.

The growth of the internal and foreign grain markets increased opportunities for the sale of agricultural products, while the development of the social division of labor and the growth of a money economy provoked a craving for the appropriation of surplus product in monetary form to an unprecedented degree . . . The process of expanded production of agricultural surplus product in *barshchina* form provoked by the conditions indicated took place, within certain limits, by means of extensive expansion of the general field to which serf agricultural labor was applied . . .

Although it was taking place within the framework of serfdom, the process of expanding the field of agricultural labor was progressive to the extent that it brought new lands into cultivation. But in the long-established regions of the country the effort to increase surplus product took other forms. It was manifested above all in an increase in the absolute quantity of surplus labor gained through "direct pursuit of *barshchina* days" [Marx], the number and relative weight of which grew in Russia during the nineteenth century.

Conditionally employing analogous concepts from the sphere of capitalist economics, one may say that in the present case there occurred an increase in absolute surplus value. But the main contradiction in the growth of surplus labor and surplus product consists in the fact that an increase in relative surplus value by methods peculiar to serfdom occurred alongside the production of absolute surplus value. Not only was an increase in the absolute quantity of surplus labor to be observed, but also a reduction in necessary labor. The latter, however, was not achieved by growth in labor productivity or by production of the required product in less labor time, but by quantitative diminution of the necessary product. The facts confirming this include, first of all, the diminution of the enserfed peasants' allotments; that is, of their fundamental means of production, which, in view of the stagnant character of technology, led inevitably to diminution of the quantity of necessary product.

At the time of the tenth revision (1858),[2] one male registered serf got 4.3 *desiatinas*, on the average, in the nonblack-soil zone, and 3.2 *desiatinas* in the black-soil zone; whereas at the end of the eighteenth century a male serf on *obrok* estates got approximately 13.5 *desiatinas* of land, and *barshchina* peasants got 8 in the nonblack-soil zone and 7 in the black-soil zone.

Diminution of necessary labor and product led to worsened living conditions for the enserfed peasant, which in turn led to a sharp reduction in and subsequently a cessation of increase in the serf population. In the nineteenth century the *mechanical* accretion of the serf population also ceased.

Pressure from the *pomeshchiks* led also to the impossibility of reproducing the implements of production, a fact that could not but influence the production process on the *pomeshchik's* own field, which, as previously noted, was cultivated not only by the serf's labor but by his implements as well. A pro-

cess of *partial* separation of the direct producer from the means of production was taking place. The peasant was gradually being deprived of land and was losing the implements of production . . .

Simultaneously with the partial dispossession of peasants and appropriation of their means of production, *complete* separation of peasants from the land and from the means of production was also occurring. This was manifested in the increase in the number of household serfs and landless agricultural laborers . . . According to the eighth revision (1836),[3] the number of household serfs constituted 4.14 percent of all *pomeshchiks'* peasants, and according to the tenth revision (1858), 6.79 percent. The number of household serfs rose during the period between these revisions by more than one-half (from 914,500 male serfs to 1,467,400 male serfs). The general increase in the number of household serfs is insufficient demonstration, however, of the true depth of the process of separation of the direct producers from the means of production, which was carried out by methods peculiar to serfdom (not by capitalist methods). In the agricultural provinces the percentages of household serfs was significantly higher than the average for the country as a whole. Household serfs constituted 14 percent of the total number of *pomeshchiks'* peasants in Orel province; 15 percent in Voronezh; 21 percent in Ekaterinoslav; and 24 percent in Kursk, Kharkov, and Kherson . . .

In these circumstances, the process of separating the direct producers from the means of production became not only and not so much a point of departure for the formation and development of capitalist relations in agriculture, as a factor in the complete pauperization of the peasantry

---

[2] Periodic "revisions," or censuses, of the tax-paying population were carried out in Russia from the reign of Peter I to the time of emancipation.—Ed.

[3] The eighth revision was in fact conducted in 1833–1834.—Ed.

and its reduction to a level approaching slavery.

Whatever the absolute number of household serfs and landless agricultural laborers may have been, the tendency of the number to increase is itself an indication of a profound transformation in the fundamental relationship of feudal society. This relationship was, of course, based on feudal landed property. Whatever the concrete historical genesis of the feudal relationship may have been, the feudal lord and master assumed the capacity of landowner, and the obligation of the serf to pay rent in one form or another was related to the fact that the peasant used the land of the feudal lord. Regardless of whether the feudal relationship arose as a result of the peasant's gradual economic enslavement by the feudal lord or by means of direct compulsion, the feudal relationship in its normal form always presupposed that the enserfed peasant used land whose property title belonged to the feudal lord. Preservation of the personal dependence of the peasant without his use of the land indicates a profound transformation in feudal-serf productive relations. It signifies a step backward, rather than forward, in the development of that social form of production . . .

Relative stability in the quantity of surplus product confiscated from the enserfed peasant by the feudal lord was characteristic of the Middle Ages. The quantity of surplus product was more or less fixed and was transformed into a norm of customary law. The fixity of the amount of surplus product, which was a direct result of the routine character of production and the unchanging level of labor productivity, subsequently became a factor in the growth of labor productivity. And the result of any rise in labor productivity could be utilized for expansion of the productive apparatus. A reverse process was characteristic of Russia in the final period of the development of serfdom: a systematic increase in the amount of confiscated surplus product in the form of *obrok*. Progress in agriculture was thereby hindered. Growth of the demesne meant separation of the direct producer from the means of production and expansion of the sphere of agricultural production under the command of the feudal lord. Growth in the number of landless agricultural laborers and household serfs carried this process to its logical extreme and liquidated one of the fundamental conditions of feudal production: the possession by the direct producer of the means of production and his personal interest in the work [which he performed].

The fundamental contradiction of Russian agriculture under serfdom, in so far as it was being drawn into wide market relations, was that it was shifting to expanded reproduction of *product* without a corresponding expanded reproduction of *the factors of production* of that product. There was no growth of the serf population; there were no indications of growth in agricultural labor productivity; and yield rates were in a state of stagnation. At the same time, as Lenin remarked, production of grain for sale by the *pomeshchik* was increasing. The exportation of grain abroad was increasing. Lenin pointed out that production of grain for sale by the *pomeshchiks* was a harbinger of the fall of the old, that is, the serf, regime. It not only undermined the natural-economy foundation of serfdom, but also, by raising the level of exploitation, sharply aggravated the contradictions between the *pomeshchik* exploiters and the exploited peasants. In addition, changes in the very character of productive relations between the *pomeshchik* and the enserfed peasant were observable.

The evolution in the forms of feudal exploitation led to acute aggravation of class antagonisms in several directions. The growth of *barshchina*, linked with the diminution of the field of necessary labor, carried the antagonism between the *barshchina* peasantry and the *pomeshchik* class to its utmost extreme. To this was added the antagonism arising from the growth in the number of landless agricultural laborers and household serfs, signifying, essentially, the restoration of slavery. The increase in the number of *obrok* peasants also promoted the aggravation of contradictions between the peasants and the *pomeshchiks*. This increase was not accompanied by an increase in the quantity of labor expended on agriculture without direct compulsion. *Obrok* had begun to lose its ties with the allotment and had begun to undergo transformation into a form of surplus product created not in agriculture but in industry. Therefore the evolution of *obrok* was a factor in the aggravation of contradictions not only between the peasants and the *pomeshchiks*, but also between capitalists—who did not wish to share the surplus value produced in their enterprises with the *pomeshchik*—and the *pomeshchiks*, who were increasingly beginning to seize the surplus product created in the sphere of capitalist industry.

The crisis of the economic order of serfdom was the result of acute incompatibility between the productive relations of serfdom and the character of the productive forces. This crisis was expressed in a number of phenomena: In industry, forms of production based on serfdom revealed their complete inability to withstand competition from capitalist forms of production, and had even begun to collapse. The natural-economy tranquillity of the serf economy had been disturbed, and a striving for expanded production of surplus product, together with a simultaneous tendency toward diminution of the productive foundation of the peasant economy, was revealed. This contradiction, which kindled antagonism between the classes, could not be resolved on the basis of the productive relations of serfdom.

Until very recently, general studies of the social and economic history of prereform rural Russia relied almost exclusively on a few global statistical estimates compiled before the turn of the twentieth century. In recent years new quantitative investigations, employing computer techniques and mathematical statistics, have begun to appear. One of the leaders in this field and the first to produce a full-scale study of prereform rural Russia is I. D. KOVAL'CHENKO (b. 1923), professor of history at Moscow University. Although Koval'chenko does not depart in his general interpretation from established Soviet views, his work has led him to a novel assessment of the role of peasant farming in the development of Russian agrarian relations, as the following translation of the conclusion to his major work indicates.*

I. D. Koval'chenko

Peasant Capitalism

Study of the socioeconomic development of the Russian serf village in the first half of the nineteenth century permits several general conclusions and, in particular, a more precisely defined conception of the essential nature of the crisis in the feudal-serf economic system.

The final stage in the development of the feudal structure was the period of its *decomposition.* That period was characterized by the fact that growth of productive forces and qualitative improvements in the social division of labor had fostered the development of commodity-money relations to the point where they had begun to exercise a *determining* influence on the entire course of socioeconomic development.

On the one hand, this led to the inevitable involvement of the feudal-serf economic system in commodity-money relations. The old base began to adapt itself to the new conditions. This adaptation led, however, to the gradual alteration and undermining of the foundations necessary for the supremacy and normal functioning of the feudal-serf economic system. One of the fundamental conditions of the feudal-serf system was the prevalence of a natural economy. The development of commodity production[1] undermined the natural character of the *pomeshchik* and peasant economy. Further, the transformation of feudal rent from a consumer value into a con-

[1] *tovarnoe proizvodstvo:* production for sale; here rendered as "commodity production."—Ed.

*From I. D. Koval'chenko, *Russkoe krepostnoe krest'ianstvo v pervoi polovine XIX v. (The Russian Serf Peasantry in the First Half of the XIX Century)*. Moscow: Izdatel'stvo Moskovskogo universiteta, 1967, pp. 378–386. Footnotes omitted. Translated by Terence Emmons.

sumer-exchange value, which had been caused by the development of commodity-money relations, had led to a sharp rise in its dimensions, out of proportion to the income-producing capabilities of the peasant economy. Reduction of the peasants' productive potentialities was the inevitable result. By the same token, the foundation on which the entire system of feudal production had been erected was undermined, which fact signified the transformation of serf relations into a brake on the development of the productive forces based on those relations. Thus, internal contradictions arose in the feudal base.

On the other hand, the development of commodity-money relations, which constituted a generalized manifestation of progress in the forces of production, provided the basis for the formation of small-scale commodity and capitalist forms of social production.[2] They provided an incomparably wider scope for the development of productive forces than did feudal relations. Progressive restriction of the potentialities for development of social production on the basis of serf relations, and their successful progress on the basis of small-scale commodity and capitalist relations, were the two sides of a single process of socioeconomic development in the epoch of the decomposition of feudalism.

Russia's feudal-serf order entered the period of its decomposition prior to the nineteenth century. The question of just when this period began remains controversial to the present day. The majority of scholars postulate that the epoch of the decomposition of feudalism in Russia began approximately in the mid-eighteenth century. Further investigations will be neces-

sary before a final answer to the question can be given.

The period of decomposition of the feudal-serf economic system did not constitute an indivisible whole. Internal stages are clearly distinguishable within it: In the first stage, serf relations, although acting as a brake on the development of productive forces, *had not yet excluded the possibility of some progress on the basis of those relations.* Fundamental testimony to this was the rise in the level of the *pomeshchik* economy and of the economy most closely connected with it—that of the *barshchina* peasants—in the first decades of the nineteenth century. Moreover, the development of new relations in the initial stage of decomposition (factory production in industry and the initial steps in the transformation from a natural to a commodity economy in agriculture), although restrained by serfdom, nevertheless still fit within the framework of feudalism, and the contradictions between the old and the new had not yet grown into an irreconcilable conflict.

The situation was different in the concluding stage of the decomposition of serfdom, which was *a period of crisis* for the feudal-serf system. *The period of crisis was that stage in the decomposition of feudalism when serf relations in their entirety already excluded the possibility of the development of productive forces on their foundation; when the collapse of economic forms based on serfdom was taking place, and progress in social production was being realized on the basis of small-scale commodity and capitalist relations whose further development demanded the immediate liquidation of serfdom.*

Analysis of the Russian serf's status and the condition of his economy in the last decades of the serf epoch shows that in the final stage of the decomposition of feudalism the developmental possibilities in the village of social production on the basis of serf relations were, on the whole, exhausted, and that these relations had been

[2] The distinction to be made between "small-scale commodity" production and "capitalist" production is that between a peasant who produces for sale with his own labor only (and that of his family), and one who employs hired labor in producing for sale.—Ed.

transformed into fetters on social production. The paralyzing effect of serfdom was apparent with particular clarity in the *barshchina* village. It was there especially that, because of the extreme intensity of the exploitation of the peasants, the economic level declined and the condition of the peasants deteriorated to the greatest extent. This testified to the fact that the feudal-serf economic system had historically outlived itself. On the other hand, the course of the village's socioeconomic development shows that the last preform decades were the period of the most intensive productive and socioeconomic progress in the entire feudal epoch.

The trends of socioeconomic development characteristic of the Russian serf village were also characteristic, as has been shown in the works of Soviet scholars, of *pomeshchik* villages in other regions of the country, of the state and appanage peasants, and of industrial production. Thus, N. M. Druzhinin showed in his fundamental study that the socioeconomic development of the state village in the last decades of the serf epoch

revealed, on the one hand, a spontaneous forward movement as a result of the labor efforts of the mass of small producers with only insignificant assistance from the government; while on the other hand it encountered a multitude of barriers erected by unchecked feudal exploitation and paralyzing feudal tutelage. This profound contradiction was a fundamental manifestation of the social crisis that was corroding the doomed feudal system.

In the sphere of industrial production in the preform epoch, the crisis of estate and possessional manufacturing[3] was combined with the rapid growth of capitalist

[3] "Possessional manufacturing" was carried on in enterprises run by nongentry entrepreneurs with a peasant labor force ascribed by the state to the enterprises rather than to the person of the entrepreneur. At the time of emancipation, there were some 518,000 "possessional peasants" in Russia.—Ed.

manufacturing and the nascent industrial revolution.

Analysis of the socioeconomic development of the Russian serf village in the first half of the nineteenth century confirms the opinion that the crisis of the feudal-serf economic system in Russia became obviously and fully apparent approximately in the period of the 1830s to 1850s and reached its greatest intensity and scope by the middle of the century.

In discussing the essential nature of the crisis in the feudal-serf economic system, it is imperative to note a number of features which are still inadequately taken into consideration by scholars. First of all, it should be emphasized that the decomposition and crisis of the feudal-serf economic system was a process characteristic of the system of socioeconomic relations as a whole. Therefore, one must not judge the essential nature of the crisis of serfdom, or the correlation between the above-mentioned two sides which was characteristic of it, on the basis of data pertaining only to one or another category of peasants, branch of the economy, or region of the country. It is quite obvious that of the two types of phenomena characteristic of socioeconomic development in the crisis epoch of feudalism, the dominant and determining one was the tendency toward the progressive development of social production on the basis of small-scale commodity and capitalist relations, for in it was expressed the fundamental essence of the historical process: its ongoing, progressive character. However, the phenomena of progressive development played a leading role and were predominant only in terms of the entire system of social production. In individual spheres of economic activity and types of economies the correlation between the two tendencies could vary. This is quite apparent in the example of the Russian serf village. Features of stagnation and decline in the *barshchina* village were manifested with particular clarity in the last prereform decades. Growth of the new tendency had its greatest successes among the *obrok* peasantry, primarily craft and craft-agricultural. To the extent that *barshchina* peasants constituted the majority of the population of the serf village, phenomena of stagnation and even decline, created by the paralyzing effect of serfdom, prevailed over the progressive development of production in a number of areas of economic activity. But it certainly does not follow from this, as is sometimes thought, that the fundamental essence of the crisis and its main manifestations were expressed in stagnation and decline. The unfounded character of such conclusions consists not only in their abstraction from the fact that on the whole the tendency toward progressive development clearly prevailed at the level of social production, but also in the underestimation or even complete neglect of the fact that the two tendencies of socioeconomic development were characteristic of all basic spheres of productive activity and all regions of the country. Only their correlation varied. It has been shown above that progressive developmental tendencies of social production were broadened and strengthened even in the *barshchina* village, where the paralyzing effect of serfdom was manifested with particular force. We may note that precisely the broad involvement of the *barshchina* village in the process of ongoing, progressive development was, above all, that new feature which characterized the socioeconomic structure of the village in the crisis epoch of serfdom.

An important peculiarity of the progressive development of the village in the crisis epoch of serfdom, as is apparent from the example of the serf village (and not only the Russian village, or the serf village alone, but also the state village), was that

this progress occurred under conditions in which the economic situation and status of the bulk of the peasantry were deteriorating. Only a small stratum of peasants improved their own situation in the process of making their contribution to social progress. The bulk of the rural population contributed more than it received. This was a manifestation of the regularity of historical development, consisting of the fact that in an antagonistic society progress may be combined with a deterioration in the circumstances of its authors. In Russia this decline occurred not only in the last prereform decades, but also in the postreform epoch, when the development of capitalism in the village was accompanied by a deterioration in the economic situation and status of the peasants in a great many regions. This contradictory nature of historical development is not always taken into consideration by scholars. Combined with an effort to emphasize progressive advances in the village, this leads to neglect of deteriorating peasant conditions; while in combination with accentuated attention on the deterioration of peasant conditions it leads to underestimation of the progressive development.

An acute aggravation of contradictions between the old and the new, the emergence of an irreconcilable social conflict, was characteristic of the crisis epoch of serfdom. The foundations of this conflict are often characterized one-sidedly. They are primarily perceived in the ruin of the old order—in the stagnation and decay in the branches of agricultural production and in the deterioration of the peasants' economic situation and status which occurred in the crisis period of serfdom. All this did indeed testify to the constrictive role of serfdom and led to an acute aggravation of class antagonism. This was, however, only one side of the process. The social conflict was engendered not exclusively, and indeed not so much, by the collapse of the economic forms of serfdom as by the extreme aggravation of contradiction between the new and the old, by the fact that the new had attained such a level in its development that its further growth became incompatible with the predominance of serfdom. In relation to the sphere of industrial production, this is quite obvious. As Soviet scholars have correctly emphasized, the introduction of machines, signifying the advent of an era of unprecedented successes in the development of the productive forces of society and leading to radical social changes, was incompatible with the serf order. But the beginning of the industrial revolution was only one of the most striking manifestations of those advances in the development of the new which could not be combined with the old and which therefore engendered an irreconcilable social conflict. There were also other progressive advances, less intense but incomparably greater in scale, engendering this conflict. These advances were occurring in the village and, as analysis of the socioeconomic relations in the Russian serf village shows, they were expressed in the development of productive forces and new organizational forms of social production.

An important characteristic of the development of productive forces in the village of the serf epoch, as yet inadequately appreciated by scholars, was that it proceeded first and foremost through increased labor productivity resulting from improvement of work habits based on the social division of labor and specialization of production. Production techniques and technology did not as such undergo significant changes, nor could they have until completion of the industrial revolution. The fundamental manifestation of progressive advances in the socioeconomic structure of the village was the appearance of the system of small-scale peasant commodity production which, depending on the extent of its development, had grown into capitalist production.

Both the growth in productive forces and the development of new organizational forms of agricultural production were taking place on a particularly significant scale precisely in the last decades of the serf epoch. During this period they attained such a level of development that their incompatibility with the predominance of feudal-serf relations was revealed. Feudal methods of allotting land to the peasants, extremely high intensity of serf exploitation and its extension to spheres of peasant economic activity whose foundations were nonfeudal, lack of freedom in economic activity and absence of legal rights for the peasants—all this not only restricted the growth of productive forces and hindered the transformation of small-scale commodity production in the village into capitalist production, but also became a barrier to the widespread establishment and development of *small-scale commodity production* itself. The latter situation must be emphasized because the development of small-scale commodity production was the fundamental expression of productive and social advances in the village, as well as because it is as yet insufficiently appreciated by scholars.

If the first trend in the conflict—restriction of the possibilities for transforming small-scale commodity relations into capitalist ones—was manifested to the greatest extent in the *pomeshchik's obrok* village (and also in the state village), the second—paralysis of the process of establishing small-scale commodity production—was characteristic primarily of the *barshchina* village; that is, of the fundamental mass of the enserfed peasantry. The buying and selling of land, formation of centers of commercial agriculture, emergence of peasants with sufficient means for the organization of capitalist production and of a stratum of largely expropriated peasantry—all this, while not yet determining the socioeconomic character of the *obrok* village, had already created relatively broad foundations for the transformation of small-scale commodity production into capitalist production. Under these conditions, the basic factor hindering the establishment of capitalist relations in the village was serfdom. In the *barshchina* village, the conflict between the old and the new arose on different foundations. The *barshchina* form of exploiting the peasants preserved the natural-patriarchal features of the peasant economy. It permitted the commercialization of only a part of the labor product and excluded the development of extensive small-scale commodity production for the large majority of peasants.

Thus, in the final stage of the decomposition of serfdom, in the crisis epoch, there was revealed not only the impossibility of further progress on the basis of serf relations, but also the incompatibility between the predominance of serfdom on the one hand, and the developmental level of productive forces which had been attained in both industry and agriculture, and the new organizational forms of social production on the other. The contradictions between the old and the new, which had arisen in the first stage of the decomposition of serfdom, grew into the most acute social conflict. Toward the middle of the nineteenth century the objective socioeconomic foundations for the liquidation of feudal-serf relations had been laid, and the destruction of the serf order had become a historical necessity.

Perhaps the most important characteristic of the socioeconomic development of the village in the epoch of the decomposition and crisis of the feudal-serf system in Russia was that the basic producer of agricultural products, the vehicle of progressive advances, and, at the social level, the most rational organizational form of agricultural production was the peasant economy. In the first place, by far the largest share of gross output in all basic branches of agricultural production in the last preform decades was produced by the peasant economy proper (in all its class categories). Thus, in the 1840s and 1850s, nearly 75 percent of all grain crops and potatoes was produced by the several categories of peasants. Secondly, the peasant economy was, taken as a whole, the main supplier of commodity production: in the mid-nineteenth century, the peasant economy contributed more than 40 percent of the total quantity of grain for sale, the greater part of commercial production of livestock, and almost the entire commercial harvest of such crops as flax, hemp, and sunflowers and of fruits and vegetables as well. Thirdly, labor productivity in the preform peasant economy was much higher than in the *pomeshchik* economy based on *barshchina* labor. Consequently, the peasant economy was the most rational organizational form of commodity agricultural production. And finally, the peasant economy contained significantly more internal stimuli and foundations for the establishment and development of rural capitalism and created an incomparably broader base for it than did the *pomeshchik* economy. Depending on the level of its development, the small-scale commercial production of the peasants was inevitably being transformed into capitalist production.

Thus, the broad objective-historical development of small-scale commodity production in the village and its transformation into capitalist production fully corresponded to the interests of social progress. Under the predominance of serfdom, however, the peasant economy was far from able to reveal all its potentialities for the development of productive forces and new organizational forms of social production. For this, the complete liquidation of serf relations was required.

The peculiarities in the development of the peasant economy in the crisis epoch of serfdom which are indicated above have been noted previously, to one or another degree, by Soviet scholars, but the necessary conclusions have not been drawn from them. That the peasant economy was the most rational and on the whole the dominant form of commodity agricultural production resulted in a number of important peculiarities in the historical development of our country. These were revealed first in the peasant reform of 1861. It was precisely the fact that the peasant economy constituted an independent and leading sector of commodity production which made a landless emancipation of the peasants impossible. In its socioeconomic essence, the reform of 1861 represented an intermediate variant in agrarian transformations. On the one hand, it preserved and broadened the foundations of the bourgeois-*pomeshchik* ("Prussian") path of bourgeois agrarian evolution; on the other hand, it preserved the peasant economy as an independent form of social production; that is, it did not eliminate the foundations of the bourgeois-peasant ("American") path of agrarian development, although it

did severely restrict the possibilities for such development. In short, the reform of 1861 was, on the whole, a historical compromise, reflecting the peculiarities of the socioeconomic structure of the village in the prereform epoch.

The extremely progressive historical role of the peasant economy and the restricted possibilities for its successful development constituted the objective basis of the fact that in Russia the agrarian-peasant question was the fundamental social question. The struggle over the two paths of bourgeois agrarian development for the country was, in the course of the prereform epoch and of the entire postreform epoch, a most important question in the class and sociopolitical struggle.

Finally, the fact that in Russia, as nowhere else in Europe, a revolutionary-democratic ideology, reflecting the class interests of the peasants and cast in the form of peasant utopian socialism, received wide circulation was also conditioned by the leading role of the peasant economy.

Thus, important peculiarities in the historical development of our country were conditioned, not only in the prereform period, but in the postreform period as well, by the character of agrarian relations in the crisis epoch of serfdom and by the leading role of the peasant economy in the socioeconomic development of the village.

The transition from questions of broad socioeconomic trends to questions of specific political acts and individual motivations is rarely made smoothly. In this selection, attention is turned to the most important individuals and institutions involved in preparation of the reform. The author, HUGH SETON-WATSON (b. 1916), professor of Russian history, School of Slavonic and East European Studies, University of London, provides an assessment of the reform process in the tradition of liberal Russian scholarship, in an excerpt from one of the most recent of his many works on Russia and Eastern Europe.*

Hugh Seton-Watson

Preparation of the Reform

The Decision to Abolish Serfdom

The climate of opinion on serfdom had been developing slowly towards emancipation. The stifling atmosphere of the last years of Nicholas' reign had prevented open discussion, but the war had stimulated serious thinking. The majority of landowners were still opposed to change, but for the most part ineffective in the expression of their views. It was the reforming minority of landowners that were most articulate, and it is their opinions which are most accessible to historians. Among them humanitarian considerations were certainly important. An eminent example is the Slavophil landowner A. I. Koshelyov.

A memorandum written by him for the Tsar early in 1858, while using arguments of economic self-interest, also claimed that the landowners themselves were ceasing to believe that they had a moral right to own other human beings like chattels. Koshelyov's last argument, to which he gave greatest emphasis, was that serfdom demoralizes the landowners themselves: "This measure," he wrote, "is more necessary for the welfare of our class itself even than for the serfs. The abolition of the right to dispose of people like objects or like cattle is as much our liberation as theirs: for at present we are under the yoke of a law that destroys still more in us than in the serfs any human quality."

*From Hugh Seton-Watson, *The Russian Empire, 1801–1917.* Oxford, Eng.: The Clarendon Press, 1967, pp. 334–346. By permission of The Clarendon Press, Oxford. Footnotes omitted.

During the last years the conscious desire of the serfs themselves for liberation had grown stronger. They themselves talked more freely of it, more clearly expected it. The beginning of a new reign was, as in the past, regarded as the opening of a new era. The number of local riots had notably increased since the 1840's. Their importance can be exaggerated: it is too much to speak of a revolutionary peasant movement in these years. The riots were not big enough to threaten the fabric of the state. Nevertheless, they worried the provincial governors and gendarmes, they frightened the landowners, and the reports which reached St. Petersburg were taken seriously in the ministries. They were also used as arguments for reform by independent persons like Koshelyov, Samarin, or the historian K. D. Kavelin.

The riots were taken more seriously because they coincided with the lost war. The war showed the appalling backwardness of Russia, and its dependence on the loyalty of the peasant soldier. This loyalty would not last for ever if nothing were done for the serfs. It was believed in St. Petersburg that the commander-in-chief in the Crimea, Prince Michael Gorchakov, had urged the Tsar that peace provided the chance to deal with internal problems, and that "the first thing is that we must emancipate the serfs, because this is the knot which binds together all the things that are evil in Russia."

The war also showed the desperate state of Russian communications. The economic as well as the strategical need for railways was more fully understood. The striking fluctuations of grain prices in recent years had caused hardship to both landowners and serfs. Better communications would make it possible for Russian cereals to enter the world market and bring more regular income to the agricultural population. But the railway age, and the penetration of the money economy into the Russian village, were not compatible with the survival of serfdom.

Alexander was subject to liberal influence in his closest circle. His brother Constantine had become an ardent supporter of emancipation. Possibly even more effective was his aunt, the Grand Duchess Elena Pavlovna. Always a liberal, she had yet enjoyed the affection of Emperor Nicholas. Her magnificent work for the wounded during the war had increased her standing in Russian public life. Her palace was a centre of liberal ideas, and she herself gave her protection to liberal officials such as N. A. Milyutin. The influence of these two members of the Imperial family is not so well documented as that of the officials who carried out the reform, but it cannot be doubted that it was very great. The experts prepared the legislation, but it was largely due to the advice of Constantine and Elena that the Tsar was induced to force it through.

The first indication of the Tsar's intentions was a speech to the nobility of Moscow on 30 March 1856, in which occurred the striking phrase: "It is better to abolish serfdom from above than to wait until the serfs begin to liberate themselves from below." Alexander appointed a secret committee to examine the problem. Its chairman was Prince A. F. Orlov, the former head of the Third Department under Nicholas I and now president of the Council of State. Though responsible for the repressions of the preceding reign, he was less unpopular than his predecessor Benckendorff, perhaps because he was of purely Russian origin and descended from Catherine's favourite. He possessed "that half-European half-Asiatic lordly arrogance which had so recently produced among us a kind of powerful magic charm." He was strongly conservative. The two most active reactionaries were Count

Panin, who joined the committee some months later, and M. N. Muravyov, Kiselyov's successor as minister of state properties. Muravyov was involved with his brother and cousin in the Decembrist conspiracy but had escaped punishment and made a good career. Already in 1830 he is said to have made the remark that he was "not one of the Muravyovs who get hanged, but one of those who do the hanging." This he certainly proved in Lithuania in 1863. Meanwhile he used his great abilities and energy to impede emancipation. The committee also included General Y. I. Rostovtsev. He too was regarded as a reactionary, and was distrusted by liberals because as a young man he had denounced the Decembrist conspiracy to the authorities, but he now proved to be a reformer. The most liberal members of the committee were Count Bludov, former minister of the interior and now head of the Second Department of the Imperial Chancery, General Chevkin, the minister of communications, and Count Lanskoy, the new minister of the interior. The latter was seventy-six years old. As a young man he had been a member of the Union of Virtue, but had not been involved in the Decembrist conspiracy. He genuinely worked for emancipation, and stood up for his subordinates in the ministry who were mainly responsible for the reform.

The Tsar himself opened the first meeting on 3 January 1857. The main questions put to the committee were: whether landowners should retain ownership of the whole of their land; whether the emancipated serfs should be protected in their right to use part of the land; and whether the landowners should receive compensation only for such land as they granted to the peasants, or also for the sacrifice of their rights over the persons of their serfs. The third question was quickly decided in principle: there was to be no compensation for the loss of the person of a serf. The committee was also presented with papers prepared in the previous reign and with certain memoranda from individual landowners, including Yuri Samarin, Kavelin, and Koshelyov. The work went very slowly. In August the Tsar made his brother a member in order to speed things up. It was then decided to entrust to the Ministry of the Interior the task of collecting all necessary information and drafting proposals. The fact was that though the majority of the dignitaries in the committee were against reform, they were too uninformed and too lazy to be effective. The efficient officials of the ministry proved more than a match for them in the next years.

The Machinery of the Reform

In November the governor-general of Vilna, General V. I. Nazimov, arrived in St. Petersburg with some proposals from the Vilna nobility for emancipation of their serfs, on unfavourable terms, without granting them any land. But the Tsar, who attached importance to the co-operation of the nobility in his plans, and had been disappointed that his Moscow speech had so far failed to provoke any initiative from the landowners, seized on these proposals as a means of carrying the work an important stage further. He instructed Lanskoy to draft a rescript for Nazimov, directing the nobility to set up provincial committees in Lithuania to prepare precise proposals. These were to include the following principles. The landlords were to remain owners of the land, but the peasants were to acquire ownership, by purchase over a definite period of time, of their house and the surrounding land (*usadebnaya osedlost'*), and were also to be assured the use of further land, sufficient for their needs, in return for *obrok* or labour services. The peasants were to be allotted to village communities *(sel'skie obshchestva)*, but the landlords were to retain police powers and there were to be arrangements to ensure the payment of taxes and the discharge of local services. Two days later, on 22 November, the Tsar asked the governor of Voronezh to persuade his nobility to put forward proposals, and early in December another rescript, somewhat more cautiously phrased, was addressed to the governor-general of St. Petersburg. A few days after this it was decided to release the texts of both rescripts for general publication.

Publication compelled the provincial nobility to face the problem. During 1858 committees were set up in most provinces of Russia. They were composed of two persons elected by the nobility in each *uezd*[1] of the province, together with two further persons chosen by the provincial governor from among the local landowners. Since the governors understood that official policy now favoured reform, they usually appointed persons of markedly more reforming outlook than those elected by the nobility. Meanwhile the existence of the secret committee was revealed to the public under the name of Chief Committee on Peasant Affairs. Its members continued to disagree. In the Ministry of the Interior a special land department was set up under Y. A. Solovyov. Its draft programme of action was rejected by the committee. Instead Rostovtsev, advised by M. P. Pozen, a conservative landowner with some expert knowledge, produced a new plan, more complicated in its procedure and designed to increase the police powers of the landowners over the emancipated peasants and to minimize the amount of land to be placed at their disposal.

In June 1858 Rostovtsev took four months' leave abroad, in order to study the

material at leisure. In his absence the reactionaries proposed that special temporary governors-general should be created for the execution of the reform, on the grounds that there would be serious danger of disorders by the peasants. This was an attempt to take control of the reform out of the hands of the Ministry of Interior, of which the reactionaries were understandably suspicious. The Tsar at first approved the idea, which was vigorously opposed by Lanskoy. Alexander expressed his displeasure at the minister's objections, which he claimed to believe had been prepared "not by you but by someone or other from among your heads of department or chancery," jealous for their own petty authority. This rebuke nearly led to the resignation of Lanskoy. But the Tsar soon afterwards made it clear that he had full confidence in him, and in fact the plan to create temporary governors-general was never carried out.

The publication of the rescript led to animated discussion in the press. Even the extreme left were for a time enthusiastic. Herzen wrote in his paper *Kolokol*, published in London: "Thou has triumphed, O Galilean!" The landowners, he argued, would be helpless when they had united against them "authority and freedom, the educated minority and the whole nation, the Tsar's will and public opinion." Chernyshevsky in *Sovremennik* compared Alexander's action with that of Peter the Great, and stated: "The blessing, promised to the peace-makers and the meek, crowns Alexander II with a happiness with which as yet none of the sovereigns of Europe has been crowned—the happiness of alone beginning and completing the liberation of his subjects." *Russkii vestnik*, edited by M. N. Katkov, expressed the views of the reformers in the central industrial provinces, such as Unkovsky, the Tver marshal of the nobility, while liberal landowners from

---

[1] Provincial subdivision or district. Most provinces consisted of from eight to twelve *uezds.*—Ed.

black-earth provinces, including Samarin, Prince Cherkassky, and Koshelyov, were grouped around *Russkaya beseda*.[2] Press discussion was, however, limited by the censorship in April 1858, as a result of the publication in *Sovremennik* of an earlier memorandum by Kavelin. This had proposed not only that the peasants be completely emancipated from all authority of their landowners, but that they be enabled to become owners of all the land at present in their use. These radical proposals caused the Tsar to decide not to employ Kavelin as tutor for the Tsarevich, as had been intended, and to instruct the minister of education to order censors to confine press discussion of the problem to "learned, theoretical, and statistical articles," and to forbid any works that stirred up classes against each other.

During August the Tsar made a tour of a number of provinces, addressing the nobility in Tver, Kostroma, Nizhnii Novgorod, Vladimir, and Moscow. In Moscow he went out of his way to refute the restrictive interpretation placed by the conservatives on the meaning of the phrase *usadebnaya osedlost'*, used in the rescript. He emphasized that this meant not only the house a peasant lived in but also the land immediately surrounding it. In September he also spoke in Smolensk and in Vilna. During the summer too Rostovtsev had begun to change his ideas as he studied the facts. He became convinced that it was necessary to enable the peasants to buy more than just the plot around their homes. He wrote several letters to Alexander from Germany, and on his return to the capital found himself in close agreement with the emperor.

From then onwards he was Alexander's most trusted adviser, and his influence was definitely liberal.

A mass of material was now coming in from the provincial committees. Many committees could not agree and sent two reports—a majority view and a minority view. The main committee had in June set up a commission of four of its members—Lanskoy, Panin, Muravyov, and Rostovtsev. These were now equally divided into two factions, and in any case had not the resources to digest all the material. Rostovtsev therefore proposed that much larger sub-committees of experts be set up to examine all the papers. These were to be called the Editorial Commissions, subdivided into administrative, juridical, and financial but in fact sitting as one body. The commissions were composed of officials and of non-official experts invited by the government. Reformers were predominant.

The most important individual member was N. A. Milyutin. A nephew of Count P. D. Koselyov's and much influenced by him, he had served in the ministry since 1835. He had been responsible for the reorganization of St. Petersburg municipal government in the late 1840's and had then acquired a reputation for radicalism. Alexander II at first distrusted him. When Lanskoy introduced him to the Tsar in July 1858, the latter coldly remarked: "Il paraît que vous possédez la confiance de votre ministre; j'espère que vous saurez la justifier." Milyutin, however, was highly regarded by the Grand Duchess Elena who probably spoke to the Tsar in his favour. In the autumn he was made deputy minister of the interior but only provisionally, and only after Prince Obolensky, to whom the post was offered, had insisted that it was Milyutin's due. In the spring of 1859, when he was received in audience by the Tsar, he was told that the appointment

---

[2]*Russian Talk:* Along with *Sovremennik (The Contemporary)* and *Russkii vestnik (Russian Courrier)*, this was one of the most influential journals of the prereform period. It published a special supplement devoted entirely to the "peasant question."—Ed.

was "a chance for him to rehabilitate himself."

The most influential of the non-official experts were the Slavophil landowners Samarin and Prince Cherkassky. Milyutin wrote to Samarin on 3 March urging him strongly to accept:

Je peux vous assurer que les bases du travail sont larges et raisonnées. Elles peuvent être acceptées en toute conscience par ceux qui cherchent une régulière et pacifique solution du problème du servage. Rejetez toute méfiance à ce sujet et arrivez hardiment. Sans doute nous ne serons pas sur des roses; nous serons vraisemblablement en butte à la haine, à la calomnie, à des intrigues de tout genre; mais pour cela précisément, il nous est impossible de reculer devant la lutte sans trahir toute notre vie passée.[3]

Both Samarin and Cherkassky accepted. Koshelyov had hoped to be invited but was not called upon.

The Emancipation

The Editorial Commissions began work in the spring of 1859. The two main problems before them were, first, how much land was to be given to the peasants and on what terms, and secondly, what kind of administrative authority was to take the place of the powers of the serf-owning landlord.

On the first problem there were several possibilities. One was to give the peasant full personal freedom but no land. This had been done by the German landowners in the Baltic provinces under Alexander I. The result had been to create a rural land-less proletariat. Such a prospect was not displeasing to some black-earth landowners in well-populated regions. But it was anathema to the Russian authorities who were obsessed with the dangers of creating a proletariat. A second possibility was to let the peasants have the use of part or all of the land they now cultivated, while leaving the property rights over it to the landowner. This is what had been done in the Baltic provinces in the 1840's, when the evil results of the earlier reform had been mitigated by instituting what was called *Bauernland,* a portion of the estates which remained the property of the landowners but was guaranteed in use to the peasants. One suggestion was that such land should be made available to the Russian peasants only for a limited period (twelve years) and then revert unconditionally to the landowners. Another was that it should pass permanently into peasant use, but in a quantity considerably smaller than that at present cultivated by the serfs. A third was that it should pass permanently into peasant use in the existing quantity. Samarin suggested that the present allotments should be a minimum, and that in regions of dense population they should where possible be increased. In sparsely populated areas, however, there might be a case for reducing the allotments to a maximum size per peasant family, the landowner to have unconditional ownership of the excess. The problem also arose whether the peasants should have the right to buy, over a period of time, the land that was ensured for their use, and if so on what terms. As we have seen, Rostovtsev had moved from the original idea of a small *usadebnaya osedlost'* (never very clearly defined) to that of agricultural allotments sufficient to support a whole family. It still, however, had to be decided what rent or labour services would be paid for such land, and at what point (after how many

---

[3] "I can assure you that the conditions of the work are broad and well thought out. They can be accepted in good conscience by those who seek an ordered and pacific solution to the problem of serfdom. Reject all suspicion on that account and come confidently. We shall probably not have an easy time of it. We shall very likely be the object of hatred, calumny, and intrigues of all kinds. But precisely for that reason we cannot retreat before the battle without betraying all that we have lived for up to now."—Editor's translation.

years of "temporary obligation") purchase should begin.

On the second problem the first question was, would the peasants become genuinely free citizens, or merely have their servitude to the landlord replaced by subjection to another bureaucratic authority. Connected with this was the question, to what extent would the landlord, no longer a serf-owner, reappear in a new guise as head of the local police authority. Inevitably, the administrative system instituted by Kiselyov for the state peasants became a model. Some of the leading non-official experts (for instance Samarin, Cherkassky, and Koshelyov) were influenced by Slavophil romanticism about the peasant commune. Self-governing communes, they felt, should be the main organ of government. Moreover, these communes should be responsible not only for taxation and public works but also for the whole process of transfer of land to the peasants and for the organization of agriculture. These men were strongly opposed to basing agriculture on individual small farmers. Not the individual but the commune ought to be both the social and the economic unit of Russian society. The landowners were keen to assert their authority and wished that the *sel'skoe obshchestvo,* the lowest level of administration, should be based not on the village commune but on the boundaries of the landowner's estate. There might thus be more than one *sel'skoe obshchestvo* affecting the inhabitants of one village, and one *sel'skoe obshchestvo* might contain persons from several villages.

The conflict of views between landowners and bureaucrats was not a simple clash between reactionary serf-owners anxious to retain privileges and a progressive government trying to help its subjects. This clash of course existed. But there was also another conflict: between reforming landowners who wished the new régime to al-

low elected self-government, and ultimately a liberalization of the whole political system, and reforming bureaucrats who were convinced that only a benevolent autocracy could do good. It was the familiar argument between the social *élite* and the central power, which had been so prominent in Russian political thinking since the beginning of the nineteenth century. It came to the surface during the discussions between the Editorial Commissions and the deputies of the provincial committees of the nobility, who came to St. Petersburg in two groups in August 1859 and January 1860.

Milyutin had no sympathy for the aspirations of constitutionally minded landowners. A memorandum of Lanskoy to the Tsar of August 1859, inspired by Milyutin, claimed that the government's main care must be to prevent "the opinions expressed in a scattered fashion in the various committees from fusing together into like-thinking parties of various hues, which have not yet formed, and which would be harmful both for the government and for the people." It must be made clear to the deputies that they were being invited to clear up points of detail concerning the special circumstances of their regions, not to discuss the basic principles of the reform, or the application of those principles "which is the prerogative of the government itself." The nobility had, however, expected that the deputies of provincial committees would be allowed to do more than this: such had been their impression of the Tsar's own intentions, as expressed in his speeches in the summer of 1858. The first group met in the house of Count Peter Shuvalov in St. Petersburg, and drew up a letter to Rostovtsev, for transmission to the emperor, signed by twenty-eight persons. The reply was that the emperor agreed to the deputies meeting to discuss their common problems, but that such meetings could have no official character. They must confine themselves to discussing the application to their particular conditions of the general principles that had been already accepted and not discuss the principles themselves. They were assured that all their replies would be put before the chief Committee as well as the Editorial Commission. On 4 September the Tsar met the deputies at Tsarskoe Selo and made them a short speech in which he declared: "I considered myself the first nobleman when I was heir to the throne, I took pride in this, I take pride in it now, and do not cease to consider myself as belonging to your estate." The deputies were not, however, satisfied by this compliment. Eighteen of them signed an address to the Tsar, which was a modified version of a draft prepared by Koshelyov. In it they asserted that the proposals of the Editorial Commissions did not correspond to general needs and did not embody the general principles which the nobility had accepted. They asked for permission to submit their views on the final work of the Editorial Commissions before the latter went before the Chief Committee. Another address, signed by five persons, put forward a whole democratic political programme. The serfs were to receive full liberty and full ownership of their land by purchase "at a price and in conditions not ruinous for the landowners." A system of economic and executive administration, equal for all classes, was to be set up on the elective principle. There was to be an independent judiciary, with trial by jury, separation of judicial and administrative power, publicity of court procedure, and responsibility of officials to the courts. Finally, the public was to have the opportunity through the press to bring to the notice of the supreme power "deficiencies and abuses of local administration." These addresses infuriated Alexander, who objected to any sort of criticism,

and to any participation by non-official representative bodies in the reform. Though some of the demands of the address of five were later granted, the Tsar refused to discuss them at this stage. The signatories of both addresses received official rebukes.

The work of reform suffered a serious blow when Rostovtsev died in February 1860. Alexander appointed Panin in his place. Though himself an undoubted reactionary, Panin did not much influence the further course of the work, and he accepted Milyutin and the liberals loyally as his collaborators. The second group of provincial deputies came mostly from black-earth regions. They did not, like the first group, make demands of a political nature, but they were hostile to the commissions, which they regarded as far too favourable to the serfs. The commissions' chief expert for the south-western area, Samarin, was under heavy attack but stood up for himself vigorously. He wrote at this time to Koshelyov: "Their remarks were full of accusations (against us) of communism, and of a concealed desire, by annoying the nobility, to deprive the throne of its foundation."

There was undoubtedly bitter hostility between landowners and bureaucrats, and the bureaucracy was itself divided between reformers and reactionaries. The Ministry of the Interior was the stronghold of the liberals. Harried by the intrigues and calumnies of the reactionaries, the liberals increasingly treated the landowning class with contempt, though they themselves derived from it. The moderate reformer A. I. Levshin believed that they had become determined to crush and humiliate the landowners, and that this harmed their cause. The bitterness of the reactionary party was vividly expressed in a memorandum by N. A. Bezobrazov, addressed to the Tsar in 1853. The author argued that "around the throne the bureaucracy is on guard, in complicity (consciously or unconsciously) with the so-called Reds." The revolutionaries had learnt from their previous mistakes, and were now busily penetrating the government machine.

Secretly promoting each other, they have got control of some branches of the administration, they have first seized certain posts which are not obvious to outside view but are absolutely essential, they have moved up higher still, and now they are using the force of the government to do what their predecessors wished but were unable to achieve.

This memorandum was treated with contempt by the Tsar. Another example was Count D. N. Tolstoy, a landowner and former provincial governor and high official of the Ministry of the Interior. In his memoirs many years later he wrote that there were at this time two parties in Russia. One consisted of sincere supporters of reform who desired a peaceful settlement of the serf problem in the interests of Russia's national greatness.

The majority of this party consisted of noble landowners, and in the conditions of St. Petersburg public life there was practically no trace of their influence in the capital. The other party was numerous, powerful, and invincible in St. Petersburg, and had its sympathizers in the provinces too. It consisted exclusively of officials, writers, and journalists. I shall not be far wrong if I call it the Red party.

The commissions' work was concluded in October 1860. The Tsar then appointed Grand Duke Constantine as chairman of the Chief Committee, which was responsible for preparing the final proposals. The experts in practice remained as an unofficial advisory group consulted by the grand duke and by the liberal members of the Chief Committee. Alexander himself pressed the committee to act quickly. In January 1861 its proposals were rapidly discussed in the Council of State, and on 19 February the statutes were signed, introduced by a rhetorical manifesto drafted by Metropolitan Filaret of Moscow.

Since 1958, a group of Soviet historians has devoted a number of volumes to study of the political, social, and ideological struggle surrounding the Emancipation of 1861. The leader of this group is Academician M. V. NECHKINA (b. 1901), like N. M. Druzhinin a major figure in Soviet historiography of nineteenth-century Russia. A specialist on the revolutionary movement whose works include a monumental study of the Decembrist Rebellion of 1825, Academician Nechkina has sought to provide methodological and theoretical foundations for the work of this group by recourse to the concept of the "revolutionary situation" as elaborated by Lenin. Her prescription on how the emancipation should be approached in accordance with this concept is included in the following article.*

M. V. Nechkina

The Reform as a By-product of the Revolutionary Struggle

"Reforms are a by-product of the revolutionary struggle." The application of this well-known Marxist proposition to the reform of 1861 belongs to V. I. Lenin. In one of his works especially devoted to the peasant reform, Lenin also dwelt upon the general theoretical content of this deduction, analyzing the role of revolutionaries in the process of social development: ". . . Revolutionaries played a very great historical role in social struggle and in all social crises, *even when* these crises led directly to only partial reforms. Revolutionaries are the leaders of those social forces which create all transformations . . ." Further on there follows the formulation cited above on reforms as a by-product of the revolutionary struggle . . .

Analyzing Lenin's legacy, we cannot but conclude that the preconditions for the reform of 1861 and the very process of its preparation were understood by Lenin as an extremely intricate complex of phenomena. Their interdependence is evident with particular clarity, for example, in the work "The Peasant Reform and the Proletarian-Peasant Revolution."

Examining the preconditions for the reform, Lenin points to:

The force of *economic development* which compelled advocates of serfdom to undertake reform (Lenin gives first priority to an analysis of basic phenomena). The nature of the progressing forces of production came into sharp conflict with the old relations of production.

---

*From *Revoliutsionnaia situatsiia v Rossii v 1859–1861 gg.* (*The Revolutionary Situation in Russia in 1859-1861*). Moscow: Izdatel'stvo Akademii Nauk SSSR, 1962, pp. 7, 9–10, 14–17. Footnotes omitted. Translated by Erica Brendel.

The *mass movement* (an increase in the number of peasant "rebellions" with every decade) developing on this foundation.

The force of the *revolutionary movement,* which represented peasant interests and reflected in its ideology the demands of the peasant masses.

The *state superstructure* cracks and falters under the resultant conditions of general national crisis: the masses do not want to live in the old way—the ruling circles cannot govern in the old way. The "rottenness and impotence" of tsarist Russia under serfdom, already exposed by the Crimean War, developed into a "crisis of the ruling circles." Together with this crisis and within it, a crisis of government policy was growing.

A "crisis of the ruling circles," a "crisis of ruling class policy"—according to Lenin—is one of the main symptoms of a revolutionary situation. It expresses the inability of the ruling classes "to maintain their supremacy in immutable form." The "ruling circles" can no longer live in the old way. In literature on the revolutionary situation, this aspect of the question is the least explored; nevertheless Lenin, as we know, began his analysis of the question precisely with this; he placed it foremost in his well-known theoretical analysis of the problem of the revolutionary situation, included in the work "The Failure of the Second International."

The "crisis of the ruling circles" and the "crisis of ruling class policy" are linked together in the most profound manner; they are, rather, internally fused. But all the same, in our opinion, they are not completely identical. Pertaining to a single complex phenomenon, they characterize its various aspects. The "crisis of the ruling circles" applies to the ruling class as a whole and characterizes its objective position in the class struggle of the period. It manifests itself in the entire stream of ideo-

logical phenomena which expresses recognition by the ruling class of the revolutionary situation, its struggle with the crisis, and its attempts to adjust to new objective circumstances, aimed at preservation of its class supremacy under new conditions of social process. The entire intricate complex of these conditions gives rise directly to a crisis of government policy in the true sense of the word—a crisis produced by these conditions and constituting a rather more special phenomenon, expressing itself above all in some kind of system of concrete *actions* by the government, of government measures—be it an intricate complex of new *laws,* altering the position of entire social classes, or particular decrees on the obligatory matriculation of students, the dispersal of some demonstration, the crushing of a peasant uprising, the arrest of a participant in the revolutionary movement, his investigation and trial. Of course, all such government measures reveal, together with a crisis of government policy, the "crisis of the ruling circles" which is characteristic of it. But at the same time they pertain to a special, narrower sphere of real government measures, which differentiates them from the broader range of various social manifestations of crisis in the ruling class as a whole. The gentry project for resolution of the peasant question belongs to the "crisis of the ruling circles," while the "Statutes" of February 19, 1861, which very clearly demonstrate a "crisis of the ruling circles," at the same time represent a fundamental government measure adopted by the authorities under crisis conditions, and are the most striking manifestation of a "crisis of government policy" during the years of revolutionary situation. The reform of 1861 is an indication of the fact that the government could not rule in the old way.

The "crisis of the ruling circles," the crisis of ruling class policy, also creates, in

Lenin's words, that breach "into which the discontent and resentment of the oppressed classes force their way."

Thus, the discontent and resentment of the oppressed classes, forcing their way into the newly formed "breach," arise above all upon a profound economic basis—in this case, upon a crisis in the feudal and serf system as a whole. This is the fundamental principle of the growth of mass action, of the manifold impact of the peasantry upon the *pomeshchik* class. The lower strata do not want to live in the old way. Revolutionary democrats—ideological spokesmen for the peasantry—express its demands. Therefore it is understandable why Lenin attributed such significance to the interdependence between revolutionary activity and the reforms extracted from the governments . . .

In connection with what has been set forth above, Soviet literature should, in our opinion, considerably extend its understanding of the preconditions and process of the reform, giving greater strength to the enumerated new historiographical elements. In our opinion, the following should be broadly and distinctly applied to a treatment of the problem:

A characterization of the *revolutionary struggle* as a real force exerting influence on the course of events and extracting reform from the government.

A characterization of the reform itself as a component part of the *crisis of the "ruling circles"* and the *crisis of government policy*. It must be indicated not only that "the masses do not want" (this comes to light in a characterization of the mass movement), but also that "the ruling circles cannot" govern in the old way. The reform of 1861 must also be understood by the reader of historical works as a government *retreat* before the impact of the *peasant movement* and the *revolutionary struggle* which reflected the demands of that movement.

The reform of 1861 is a manifestation of a "crisis of the ruling circles" and a crisis of government policy. At the same time, as significant as it may be in itself, the reform nevertheless is not the only phenomenon associated with that crisis. Indeed the crisis had, in those same years of revolutionary situation, many additional aspects: at that time definite stages were being reached in the preparation of other reforms—legal, censorial, educational, and military—and not only these familiar complexes. We have before us manifestations of crisis in the entire previously adjusted bureaucratic system of tsarist administration and local and central institutions, in the entire system of class legislation. This should not only be presented as the factual fabric of a historical account (as has already been partially done in the work of M. N. Pokrovskii), but should also be *generalized* as a "crisis of the ruling circles," a crisis of government policy. The question of the crisis as a whole has not yet been posed by Soviet historical science as a special problem for study. It is important to show graphically, to give concrete expression to the conclusion that the reform of 1861 was a striking and extremely important element of that crisis.

It seems to us that the reform has been treated in a much narrower and more isolated manner. It has been torn out of its complete historical context and a certain self-sufficient character has been attached to it. Treating it somewhat in isolation, historians have not placed it in that complex system of elements enumerated above, a system to which it belongs organically, and the combination of whose elements constituted the revolutionary situation which had been created in the country.

It is natural that in a historical exposition the analysis of government measures should follow the analysis of the mass movement and the revolutionary struggle of the corresponding period and not precede it. Otherwise, Lenin's proposition that the masses *do not want to live in the old way* (which the mass movement and revolutionary struggle indeed express)—and by virtue of this, as a result of this, the ruling circles *cannot* govern in the old way—will not be taken into account, and the methodological requirements which follow from it will not be observed.

A partial, but, in our opinion, absolutely obligatory requirement is the reconstruction in precisely this order of the real historical context in which the government measures proceeded. This very simple condition of historical sequence is not observed to this day in Soviet literature of a general nature devoted to the reforms, although it has long been considered obligatory for a multitude of other problems.

Let us pause, as an example, on several well-known moments in the very process of the reforms, a subject which is now considered the most fully explored aspect of the abolition of serfdom. Both the speech of the tsar at his meeting with the Moscow gentry in 1856 and the rescript to Nazimov in 1857 are, as a rule, presented in isolation from the social movement and the peasant struggle. Let us apply the above-mentioned generally accepted requirement to them.

An account of Alexander II's address to the Moscow gentry with the words that it is better to liberate the peasants from above than to wait until they begin to liberate themselves from below must obviously be prefaced by an account of real peasant disturbances *on the eve* of that address, as well as by information on the revolutionary struggle of the time. Then the government action is placed in its real context. Of course, that action was not called forth by precisely those particular events, constituting only a part of the whole picture of the movement, which occurred on

the eve. It was dependent upon the major, protracted, recurrent phenomena which have already been discussed above—the economic structure of the epoch of the crisis of feudalism, the struggle of the masses, the entire preceding revolutionary movement, and the "crisis of the ruling circles." However, it is further explained, and is more distinctly delineated, by a reconstruction with the proper methodological consistency of its most immediate context. How is it possible not to recall at this point that for two whole years prior to the tsar's words—since the spring and summer of 1854—the peasant movement had been spreading as a consequence of the call-up of the State Reserves? Thousands of peasants, as we know, were stirred into action, entire villages vanished, with a fundamental goal in mind—to gain freedom at last. The call-up of the Naval Reserves (1854) roused more than ten provinces and, although it concerned only the provinces of Petersburg, Olonetsk, Tver, and Novgorod, even rocked the provinces of Penza and Riazan. In the following year, the formation of the "State Mobile Reserves" roused the provinces of Voronezh, Samara, Kazan, Perm, Simbirsk, Riazan, and Chernigov. The most significant event of the movement—the "Kiev Cossack movement of 1855"—astounded contemporaries by its scope. It began just a year before Alexander's speech to the Moscow gentry and, evidently, the widespread departures of Ukrainian peasants wanting to join the ranks of the "Cossacks" and demanding freedom, as well as the bloody executions of participants in the "Cossack movement," were still fresh in the tsar's memory. Not until May 1855 was the movement drowned in blood, flogged to death with birch rods. The tsar's statement "It is better that these changes be made from above than from below"—acquires, in this context, a very real content. Why, then, do general works on the reform not recon- struct this "context" of the tsar's words? Why do they attribute to them some sort of self-sufficient character?

Just a month after the tsar's above-men- tioned aphorism, which spread throughout the country and became firmly entrenched in the literature of the problem, the gov- ernment again met with a spontaneous mass movement. In May and June of 1856 the peasants were already beginning a march "to the Crimea for freedom," seek- ing audiences in Perekop with the mythical tsar in a "golden pavilion" who dis- penses freedom to all who come; but late- comers are left as before, according to leg- end, in the power of the landowners. This movement once again roused thousands of peasants and was again put down with birch rods and bullets. Such was one as- pect of the circumstances preceding the well-known rescript of Alexander II to Nazimov on November 20, 1857. That rescript looks somewhat different if we remember the concurrent circumstances. It was also anticipated by significant events in the camp of the revolutionary move- ment—Ogarev's[1] arrival in London in 1856 to join Herzen,[2] their plan for a jour- nal with the emancipation of the peasants as its central idea, the appearance of the first numbers of *The Bell* in 1857, just prior to the rescript; and finally, the plan for creation of a nation-wide secret organiza- tion, attested to by a document written by N. P. Ogarev. The tsarist government was by no means aware of all this, but this is the objective context, essential to a histo-

rian. And this is not yet all by any means. The year 1857 was the period of the polemic between *The Contemporary* and *The Economic Handbook,* the year when N. G. Chernyshevskii[3] began his active work among the officers, his preparation and editing of the *Military Collection,* the year when Chernyshevskii's article "On new conditions of agricultural life" appeared (*The Contemporary,* 1857, no. 2). As we see, animation was evident in the camp of the revolutionary movement, the idea of a con- solidation of revolutionary forces was gain- ing ground, and the demand for liquida- tion of serfdom was a fundamental slogan. It permeated every page of *The Bell,* which "stood firm as Gibraltar for emancipation of the peasants." This is the real and still far from complete context in which the im- perial rescript of 1857 appeared. It must be agreed that it begins to look very dif- ferent here from when it is presented in isolation as some kind of result of the tsar's attempts to come to an understanding once again with the ruling class at a meet- ing of the Moscow gentry.

One can speak of the fact that on Octo- ber 10, 1860, the editing commissions completed their work and the project went on to the Main Committee on peasant af- fairs as "following" logically from preced- ing government measures. But this will sound different if we remember its objec- tive context. The situation was particularly tense. The unprecedented "sobriety move- ment" of the peasants in 1859–1860 shook the provinces. This was no longer a move- ment of the "outlying" western districts; it embraced the center of the state—the provinces of Smolensk, Riazan, Tambov, Kaluga, Kostroma, Penza, Nizhnii Novgo-

---

[1] N. P. Ogarev (1813–1877): Gentry-born poet and publicist, and life-long collaborator of Alexander Her- zen.—Ed.

[2] A. I. Herzen (1812–1870): Archtypical "gentry revolutionary," theoretician of "Russian socialism" based on the peasant commune, prolific and gifted writer and memoirist, Herzen exercised great influ- ence in Russia during the reform era through publi- cation of *The Bell (Kolokol)* in London.—Ed.

[3] N. G. Chernyshevskii (1828–1889): Radical pub- licist and theorist, and editor, until his arrest in 1862, of *The Contemporary.* By his political martyrdom and his writings, the hero of an entire generation of the Russian radical intelligentsia.—Ed.

rod. These were not sporadic outbursts of peasant anger against cruel *pomeshchiks*—something else could now be felt in the protest against government management of the "liquor monopoly." These new features, as we know, were recorded in N. A. Dobroliubov's[4] articles devoted to that movement. New features also appeared in the life of the revolutionary camp. A struggle was going on for consolidation of revolutionary forces, a program of action was being worked out. N. P. Ogarev's "Ideals" date from 1859. N. G. Chernyshevskii's visit to Herzen in London occurred in the same year. The correspondence and diary of N. A. Dobroliubov for that period obviously testify to an attempt to create a secret revolutionary organization in Russia. In 1859, on the memorable day of December 14, a public demonstration occurred during Professor P. V. Pavlov's farewell celebration before his departure for Petersburg (his toast to Herzen as a man "at the head of the progressive movement in Russia"). At the end of 1859 and the beginning of 1860 N. G. Chernyshevskii wrote his proclamation "To the manorial peasants."

Against this background—and it is still far from complete—the taking up of consideration of the editing commissions' project in the State Council appears somewhat different. Now a living fabric of interconnected events which bears a very direct relation to the collapse of serfdom in Russia is being reconstructed.

Soviet historical science differs profoundly and in principle from pre Revolutionary bourgeois science. It does not follow from this, however, that the entire complex of Leninist propositions on the reform of 1861 has been elaborated and worked out, and that there exist completely "settled," "exhausted" aspects of the problem. It seems not. Much work still lies ahead.

---

[4] N. A. Dobroliubov (1836–1861): Literary critic under Chernyshevskii for *The Contemporary,* he popularized the latter's ideas in his reviews.—Ed.

The controversy over the motivations of the reform's planners, and of Alexander II in particular, is as old as the event itself, but it is still far from settled. In this selection ALFRED J. RIEBER (b. 1931), professor of Russian history at the University of Pennsylvania, subjects a variety of explanations to critical review and offers his own interpretation, which pictures the emperor as having been moved by military considerations above all others.*

Alfred J. Rieber

Raison d'état: *Military*

The single most important event in Russian history between the reforms of Peter the Great and the revolution of 1905 was the abolition of serfdom. When, in February 1861, Alexander II signed the final act of emancipation, he sealed the doom of the old order without, however, realizing fully the tremendous impact which his action was destined to make upon the structure of the autocracy. Yet almost immediately the emancipation forced the government to introduce other sweeping reforms which in general touched upon every aspect of Russian life and, in particular, created a whole set of institutions in order to absorb the newly freed peasants into the body politic. Because the effects of the emancipation were so far-reaching many

scholars preferred to designate 1861 rather than 1917 as the watershed in modern Russian history. The proponents of this view often yielded to the natural temptation of seeking the significance of 1861 in terms of what happened in 1917. They argued, convincingly, that like the other great agrarian reforms in East Central Europe during the nineteenth century, the emancipation in Russia left behind an unresolved paradox which gradually sapped the vital forces of the state and society. The autocracy, by failing to regard industrialization as a high order of political business until late in the century, denied creative outlets to the vast energies which it had unleashed. Thus it shared the heavy responsibility for the social and economic

*From *The Politics of Autocracy. Letters of Alexander II to Prince A. I. Bariatinskii, 1857–1864*. Edited with an historical essay by Alfred J. Rieber. The Hague: Mouton & Co. n.v., 1966, pp. 15–29. Footnotes omitted.

crises of the twentieth century that shattered the political structure of East Central Europe.

However, this fascination with revolution increased the danger of finding the causes of the reform in its results, of attributing the ideas and aspirations of another generation to those who initiated the reform in a different frame of mind and under different conditions than prevailed half a century later. Consequently, some confusion has developed not only concerning the motivation for reform but also over the mechanics of its implementation.

Among the great variety of interpretations on the origins of the reforms, three schools of thought stand out. Before the revolution liberal Russian historians attributed a crucial role in launching the emancipation to the pressure of an aroused public opinion and the desire for reform which was in the air. According to most Soviet historians, the fear of mounting waves of peasant disorders forced an unwilling autocrat to grant reforms in order to head off a revolutionary upheaval. This interpretation, in modified form, has found wide acceptance in Western literature. More recently a number of American scholars have suggested that by abolishing serfdom the autocracy sought to free Russia's vast human and material resources, stimulate the economic development of the country and in a word catch up with the West. This is a more sophisticated variation of the vague thesis that the Crimean defeat exposed Russia's weakness and something drastic had to be done to correct it. Frequently, all these explanations have been lumped together as contributing factors without any effort having been made to distinguish their relative importance. Fair-minded as this last approach may seem, it really adds up to nothing more than a list of motives which might reasonably appear to have influenced those

making the decisions. While this serves a useful function by indicating the main historical problems as we see them, it is now possible to move beyond this stage and identify the issue which at the time made the decisive impression on the mind of the autocrat who was after all the sole initiator of the reform.

Just as it is desirable to narrow down the range of probable motives, so it is equally important to explain why these and not others which in retrospect may seem just as valid, persuaded the autocrat to adopt a particular course of action. Statesmen rarely act as historians would like them to, on the basis of reasoned analysis of all pertinent factors. Indeed logic in politics requires above all the willingness to re-examine long-held assumptions and the courage to revise them when they are challenged by hard facts. Thus, in seeking the underlying motives for reform, it is essential to re-examine Alexander's reaction to Russia's defeat in the Crimean War which posed a direct challenge to the long-established traditions of the autocracy.

Despite the relatively restricted area of military operations in the Crimean War, Russia's defeat was a catastrophe for the autocracy. The Russian army, which had treated East Central Europe as its own parade ground, saw its vaunted reputation crumble, burying beneath it the ruins of the conservative coalition. Defeat not only brought to an end an era of Russia's preponderance in East Central Europe but foreshadowed a period of diplomatic isolation. The autocrat himself had died suddenly in the midst of the war, broken by the repeated disasters inflicted on his beloved armies. Russian finances, which before the war had been restored to some semblance of order by Count Kankrin, were thrown back into chaos with the result that the credit of the country was shaken. Doubtless, the defeat would have compelled the autocracy to re-examine its policies even if Nicholas had survived the peace treaty. This fact was quickly realized by high government officials who, much like the Prussians after 1806, foresaw the need for a thorough overhauling of state and society. The initiation, direction and extent of these changes depended, of course, on the attitude of the new tsar, Alexander II.

At first, Alexander, although in close touch with the military situation, did not fully grasp the seriousness of his position and still hoped to salvage something from the debacle. Even after the fall of Sevastopol he spoke of beginning a new campaign in the spirit of Peter after Narva and Alexander after Borodino. For this reason he was delighted with the bold plan of his former adjutant and close friend Prince A. I. Bariatinskii to carry on the fight by withdrawing the main part of the army to the Perekop Peninsula, leaving a strong advance guard on the road to Simferopol, resting and strengthening the army behind this narrow front until it could renew the attack in spring. At the same time in the fall of 1855 he was encouraged by rumors of disorders in France which he believed might force Napoleon to sue for peace. In December Alexander was brought back to the harsh reality of his diplomatic isolation and military weakness by the Austrian ultimatum and Frederick William's ominous appeal for peace.

At two special conferences of high officials in December 1855 and January 1856, Alexander found little sympathy for continuing the war. His advisers warned that continual resistance meant certain defeat and possibly the loss of Poland and Finland as well. For the tsar it must have been even more unsettling to hear the War Minister V. A. Dolgorukov's blunt report (drafted by D. A. Miliutin) that, in comparison with Western Europe, Russia's

military, financial and industrial resources were inadequate to meet the demands of modern warfare and would completely collapse under further strain. In the face of these compelling facts, Alexander agreed reluctantly to end the fighting, accept the Austrian ultimatum as the basis for peace negotiations, and then with grave reservations sign the Treaty of Paris. The immediate pressure of a complete collapse had been lifted, but the frightening prospect of Russia's long, slow decline remained.

Alexander slowly began to recognize how radically Russia's position had been altered by defeat in the Crimean War. His elevation to the throne took place unexpectedly and at a critical moment in the war when he had little time or inclination to ponder solutions to long-range problems in the postwar period. But suddenly, contrary to his repeated assertions, he had been forced to accept terms that were incompatible with Russia's honor and status as a great power. How would he react in the face of this shocking realization? Few of his contemporaries believed he possessed the necessary courage and resolution to face the problem squarely, let alone solve it. To accept their views at face value is to question Alexander's personal responsibility for initiating the reform. Yet to deny them requires a searching answer to the question of how a reputedly weak-willed and vacillating man like Alexander could launch a fundamental reform of Russian society while his predecessor Nicholas who lacked neither the will nor possibly the desire hesitated to take this decisive step.

For insights into the tsar's character historians have traditionally relied on the memoirs of K. K. Merder and the letters of V. A. Zhukovskii, both tutors of the young grand duke. By and large they have emphasized the abundant evidence in these important sources which indicates that Alexander was a naturally well-endowed, but irresolute and indolent boy who upon encountering the slightest obstacle to his plans lapsed into a state of complete inaction. Up to a point this analysis of Alexander's character carries great weight.

Alexander was already ten years old when Merder first noted these traits. His character had been set, and despite the strenuous efforts of his tutors who enlisted the support of the emperor himself in order to stiffen his will Alexander never completely overcame this weakness. As a boy he found his studies oppressive. Nothing suited him more than to ride, hunt and enjoy the other simple pleasures of a carefree life. Once when he was rebuked for his idleness Alexander cried out in anguish, "I wish I had never been born a tsarevitch." Nor was this the last time Alexander expressed his reluctance to shoulder the burdens of the autocrat.

Nevertheless this makes up only one side of Alexander's character. After all what sustained him during the strain and tension of pushing through great reforms in the face of strong opposition from the very class upon which he relied for support? In brief it was his devotion to duty instilled into him and exemplified by his father and encouraged by his tutors. Merder was astonished to find a young man "who had such a correct view of his obligations," and he made every effort to heighten the grand duke's understanding of the historical role he was to play. Alexander was not allowed to forget that the fate of millions depended upon him. Above all it was Nicholas' stern example which overawed and inspired the boy. Nothing gave Alexander greater pleasure than to receive a word of praise from his father. Yet how often he earned only a withering rebuke for his laziness and indifference to studies. For Nicholas obedience was "a holy obligation. I can forgive anything," he told Alexander, "except a lack of sense of duty." If Alexander re-

sented this treatment he never let it be known. On the contrary he confided to his mother that Nicholas was "more than a father." "For me *he* was the *personification of our dear fatherland.*" And to his brother he added "my entire soul belongs [to him] and I will continue to serve [him] in my heart." It is noteworthy that Alexander, who was affable and kindly by nature and displayed in his family and among friends the personal charm which many have testified was irresistible, adopted in public appearances and even more under the stress of the sudden heavy responsibilities a forced solemnity and awkward majesty which distorted his features into an unbecoming mask. He then became, as Tiutcheva so aptly described him, "a bad copy" of his father. If for no other reason than to please Nicholas, Alexander worked hard as the heir to master the techniques of governing the realm. As a result, in the words of a recent biographer, he was "perhaps the best prepared heir apparent ever to ascend the Russian throne."

Deeply attached to his father and intensely aware of his obligations, Alexander fought a life-long battle against his own weak will and only gained an uncertain victory. Against his fear of irresolution he erected a wall of secrecy and stubbornness. After he had wrestled alone with his conscience and come to a decision, nothing short of a complete disaster could shake his resolution. The injustice of Valuev's quip that Alexander accepted the view of the last man with whom he spoke is revealed by the failure of Valuev to get his own ideas endorsed. Though obstinacy is a frequent but unsatisfactory substitute for real strength of character, it was enough to sustain Alexander's determination to make far-reaching changes in the face of indifference and resistance. His firm resolution during the period preceding the reform amazed his contemporaries even as they puzzled over its source and inspiration. D. A. Miliutin recalled vividly that "the tsar showed at this time such unshakeable firmness in the great state undertaking which he had personally conceived, that he could ignore the murmurings and grumbling of the clear opponents of innovation. In this sense, the soft and humanitarian Emperor Alexander II displayed greater decisiveness and a truer idea of his own power than his father who was noted for his iron will."

But what does a sense of duty mean to a man who has been taught that he is "a sacred person as the viceroy of God on earth"? Duty to what? to whom? Was there a guiding principle which gave the autocrat a sense of purpose beyond the normal tasks of safeguarding his power, protecting the church, defending the frontiers, and maintaining order? It has been shown that Nicholas's sense of duty rested on a systematic theoretical basis, but Alexander never openly endorsed that catchy slogan of Orthodoxy, Autocracy and Nationalism.

In general, Alexander regarded with suspicion all philosophical systems and ideologies, seeing even in those which embraced absolutism a threat to his freedom of action. What little interest he showed in political theory must be traced to M. M. Speranskii who at Nicholas's request delivered from 1835 to 1837 a series of lectures on law and politics to the grand duke. By his subsequent words and actions Alexander reflected Speranskii's thinking that "the private interests of a few classes do not correspond to the true interest of the whole people and often are even opposed to them." To be sure, Speranskii's appeal to true moral law as the ultimate purpose of human legislation was too vague to serve as a guiding principle. But his belief that historical tradition and undivided sovereignty provided the means to attain moral

law met a ready and practical response from Alexander. Speranskii merely confirmed that Russian autocratic thought rested on historical as opposed to rationalist foundations which, with the exception of the uncertain infatuation of Catherine and Alexander I, found little sympathy among the autocrats themselves. Once the appeal to history was sanctioned, there could be little argument that the dominant trait in Russia since Peter I was the military tradition.

To Alexander the army represented the mightiest bulwark of the autocracy, a fund of energetic and reliable advisers, a constant source of pride and pleasure. From childhood Alexander learned to extol the virtues of military training and outlook. His earliest games with toy soldiers were organized by Merder to instruct as well as amuse. Appointments to commands of crack regiments, gifts of gorgeous uniforms, participation in parades and finally field maneuvers gradually crowded out all other activities. Yet for Nicholas this was still not enough. "I have noticed," he wrote the military tutor Merder, "that Alexander shows in general little zeal for military science; I want him to know that I will not be pleased if I notice a lack of enthusiasm for this subject. He must be a soldier at heart (*voennyi v dushe*) or else in this century he will be lost; it seems to me that I have noticed he enjoys only the petty details of military life." Although Alexander never acquired his father's interest and skill in military tactics, as his letters to Bariatinskii show only too clearly, and though he permitted Zhukovskii's humanitarian sentiments to temper Nicholas' enthusiasm for combat, he lavished attention, rewards and privileges upon the army. Nor was it surprising that the military values emphasized in his education (as well as that of all the grand dukes in the nineteenth century) gave rise to a particularly rigid and harsh outlook on life. Duty, discipline, precision, order, loyalty, obedience—these were the standards by which he judged himself, his subordinates and his subjects. Frequently the result was little more than preoccupation with uniforms, decorations and parade ground drill. But to the autocracy the army was more than an expensive play-toy. It was the instrument by which Peter the Great had created the modern Russian state and secured for it a prominent place among the great powers. Lest the autocrat forget this fundamental truth of Russian history, his military advisers were always ready to remind him of it. "Thanks to the army Russia became a first class European power," Miliutin wrote to Alexander in 1867, "[and] only by maintaining the army can Russia uphold the position it has acquired." In the pre-industrial age Russia's leap to greatness had been accomplished by placing the entire population in a state of permanent mobilization. All institutions, privileges, and resources were subordinated to the needs of the army which became a political and social power in its own right. By virtue of its enormous demands upon Russia's financial, technological and productive resources, the army dominated the economy as well. In no other country with the possible exception of Prussia did the army occupy so predominant a position, and in no other country did it justify its existence with such brilliant results. Until the Crimean defeat Russia had not lost a major war in over a century and a half. Its growing role in European affairs was expressed dramatically by the appearance of Russian troops at the gates of Western capitals, Stockholm 1719, Berlin 1762, Paris 1815.

Neither Russia's industry and commerce, nor its intellectual and cultural achievements had yet earned it an honored place among the great powers. Only exploits of its army enforced Russia's claim to be a great European power. And in the nineteenth century the word European was synonymous with civilized. Great power status conferred enormous psychological and material rewards upon the recipient. Following Peter's lead the autocrats regarded Europe as the center of the world, adopted many of its ideas, attitudes and institutions, participated in its commerce, diplomacy and wars, permitted its nobles to travel widely and frequently to live for long periods in its capitals and spas. Once having fought its way into the charmed circle, Russia clung to its position tenaciously. Throughout the nineteenth century, but especially during the Crimean War, the autocrat and his advisers feared that a serious defeat in war would deprive Russia of its Western provinces (Finland, the Baltic and Polish-Lithuanian provinces) and drive the empire back into Asia. For similar reasons Alexander regarded as particularly humiliating the Black Sea clauses of the Treaty of Paris. Compulsory disarmament has not been imposed on any other country in Europe, except on Prussia after the crushing defeat of 1806, and it is hard to disagree with Taylor that "The Allies would not have presented such terms to any power whom they regarded as truly European." In the eyes of the Russian leaders it was Russia's destiny to serve as a bridge between Europe and Asia, as a civilizing force in the East. But for Russia to shift its center of gravity away from Europe into Asia was for most of them unthinkable.

Thus, when the army failed to hold its own on native soil against the West European powers, Alexander clearly saw that his duty was to reorganize the army so that it could fight on equal terms against a European coalition. Even before the war ended Alexander requested Adjutant General Count Ridiger, commander of the

Guards and Grenadier Corps, to suggest improvements in the army. Ridiger's four memoranda submitted in June 1855, pointed out a number of shortcomings such as promotion by seniority, low level of officer training and abuses of authority. He can scarcely be blamed for having avoided the fundamental issue that the army rested upon a decaying social system because his was the first criticism of the army which had been permitted in thirty years. On Ridiger's recommendation Alexander appointed in July 1855 a "special committee for the improvement of the military establishment." He had taken his first step toward the great reforms.

Among the committee's members was Prince Bariatinskii, who it appears requested the appointment in February 1856 of D.A. Miliutin, later his chief of staff and nominee for Minister of War. How closely the two men worked at the time is not known, but Miliutin submitted a detailed memorandum to the committee reaffirming the idea, already stated in the Dolgorukov memorandum, that the basic weaknesses of the existing military system were first, the absence of a territorial military organization and second, the need to maintain a large peacetime army at great expense due to the lack of a trained, combat-ready reserve such as every other continental power possessed. To correct these shortcomings, according to Miliutin, the term of service for recruits ought to be reduced to two or three years, and most of the army ought to be stationed in the inner provinces. Miliutin realized, however, that three peculiarities of the Russian Empire blocked the road to reform: the size of the country, its multinational character, and serfdom. Of these, clearly only serfdom could be altered by state action, and it was serfdom which above all prolonged the outdated military system. Not only did it complicate the task of establishing a terri-

torial organization, but in Miliutin's words, "serfdom does not permit us either to reduce the term of service or to increase the number of unlimited leaves so as to diminish the present number of troops." What Miliutin had written was common knowledge among military men of the day, but few dared to express it.

Alexander quickly came to realize that a thorough and effective army reform involved far more than carrying out Ridiger's superficial recommendations. Soon after the war, he ordered the indefinite suspension of recruiting under the old system, thereby clearing the way for a basic change in the nature of the Russian army after the emancipation of the serfs. To overcome Russia's military weakness he had to smash the rigid social system which had been created for the same reason it was about to be destroyed—to provide the state with the men and money to wage war.

The autocracy had long recognized that from the point of view of military efficiency and financial stability a trained reserve would bolster the defense of the empire, but the shock of the Crimean defeat brought home sharply the need for rapid and decisive action. During the first half of the nineteenth century Russia was forced to maintain the largest standing army in Europe, not only because of its long, exposed frontiers and the lack of a strategic railroad network, but also because in the absence of a trained reserve the army could not increase substantially its combat strength after the outbreak of war. Consequently the size of the peacetime army was to a very large degree determined by Russia's probable role in some future general European war. In light of the traditionally close association of the three eastern courts, the autocracy had every right to expect that Russia's western frontiers would be covered in case of a war against the maritime powers by at least the benevolent neutrality of Austria and Prussia. The peculiar circumstances leading to the outbreak of the Crimean War wrecked these calculations and forced the autocracy to maintain substantial forces in Poland and along the Galician frontier. As it turned out the peacetime army was unequal to the task of fighting major campaigns in the Crimea and Caucasus while at the same time defending the western frontiers against possible attack. Sobering confirmation of the fact came when the high command could muster only 100,000 men for the defense of Sevastopol, where the outcome of the war was being decided, when it had over two and one quarter million men under arms. In desperation the government resorted to extraordinary measures including unrestricted enlistments in the army and militia. These raw recruits formed new units for which of course there were no cadres, officers, supplies or equipment. They were useless for combat, a drain on the treasury and occasionally a disturbing element in the garrison towns where they were stationed.

Too inflexible to meet the demands of war, the Russian army had also become too expensive to maintain in peace. The Crimean War had absorbed more than three times the normal annual revenue of the empire and removed over one million men from the economy for three years. In addition almost 365,000 men who had been taken into the militia neither fought nor produced. This staggering cost had been only partially covered by the printing of paper money. Although Alexander was aware of the deplorable condition of Russian finances he was not prepared for the shock produced by the first peacetime budget estimates in 1857. No sooner had the budget been submitted than it was clear that the estimates of income and expenses were unrealistic. The Finance Minister ad-

mitted shamefacedly that the deficit would be twice what had been expected, almost 75 million rubles. He had drawn up the budget on the assumption that once the war was over the difficulties would end as well. But the truth of the matter was that because Russia's large standing army could not be reduced, the War and Navy Ministries had demanded 117 million of the 158 million rubles available for current expenses. Furthermore the War Ministry insisted on the allocation of supplementary emergency funds which could only be covered by printing more paper money. However, the value of the ruble was already falling rapidly.

Immediately Alexander set up a special finance committee (the first of several) to determine ways of reducing the deficit. As might have been expected, its recommendations called for nothing more imaginative than reducing expenses. The natural target was the War Ministry, but the minister N. O. Sukhozanet fought hard to restrain "the mania for savings" which threatened to disrupt many important projects. Although, as he wrote Bariatinskii, Alexander seemed determined "to cut expenses no matter what the cost even if it meant limiting our military operations [in the Caucasus] for a year or two . . .," he could not bring himself to deny his generals even greater sums. Despite the introduction of a far-reaching reorganization of Russia's financial structure based on a unified treasury, a modern budget and an independent accounting system, the military budget continued to increase and the War Minister retained control of his emergency funds. The situation could not be improved until a fundamental army reform eliminated the need for keeping such large numbers of men under arms.

As if further proof were necessary, in 1860 another special committee appointed to examine the causes for the largest deficit

since 1857 reported that the War Minister's request for an additional 16 million
rubles above his normal expenses must be
resisted. In a marginal note Alexander
wrote, "As for reducing the expenses of the
War Ministry, everything possible will be
done short of throwing the military establishment into complete disorder." As a
stopgap measure, Alexander eliminated
the fourth battalion in every regiment, but
this action brought the strong complaint
from D. A. Miliutin, the new Minister of
War, that "We lack both reserves of men
and material necessary to place our military strength on a war footing." Still, on
the eve of emancipation the military took
almost one half of the funds available for
current expenses.

In sum, while all other European states
except Britain maintained a small standing army in peacetime to hold down
costs and kept a large trained reserve ready
to expand the army in war, Russia
was saddled with the great expense of supporting an enormous permanent army
which in time of need could not be greatly
increased as a fighting force. What had
prevented the autocracy from following the
lead of the other great powers? Serfdom
blocked the path and all attempts to get
around it had failed.

Under serfdom the army was recruited
from the tax-paying population (peasant
and *meshchanin*) on the basis of five or six
per thousand for a period of twenty-five
years. Every serf who fulfilled his service
obligation left the army a free man, but
few were lucky enough to survive the long
term and those who did were hardly fit for
further military service in any capacity. In
other words they could not be expected to
form the nucleus of a trained reserve. Before the Crimean War about 80,000 men
annually entered the army and were

trained for a year in the reserve battalions.
When the next annual levy was called up,
the trainees became regular troops. As a
result there were no provisions for forming
a trained strategic reserve.

Why then did the government not reduce the term of service in order to build
up a supply of fit, trained men who could
be recalled to the colors in the event of
war? This simple expedient was fraught
with dangerous consequences. Reducing
the term of service would have greatly increased the number of annual recruits,
freed serfs at a rapid rate, and dumped a
mass of landless proletarians who were
trained in the use of firearms and military
tactics on a society which could not absorb
them. The difficulties of maintaining public order under such conditions were obvious.

Would it not have been possible to grant
unlimited leaves to a certain percentage of
the annual recruits in order to build up a
reserve? Nicholas I tried this ingenious
plan but soon discovered that without military training the serfs were useless as reserves and with training they would pose a
clear threat to the supremacy of the land-
lord-gentry whom they were bound to
serve. Miliutin had drawn the logical conclusion that Russia could not create a
trained reserve which was the backbone of
a modern European army without abolishing serfdom. Although there is no conclusive proof that Alexander followed this
line of reasoning, a mass of supporting evidence suggests that he too had come to the
conclusion that the only answer to the
need for reducing expenses while increasing the combat effectiveness of the army
was to reorganize the entire military establishment beginning with the recruiting system and that this convinced him that serfdom had to be abolished.

One of the most problematical and least understood of the questions surrounding the preparation of the emancipation is that of the economic expectations of its planners. A thoughtful investigation of this question is provided by ALFRED A. SKERPAN (1914–1968), late professor of history at Kent State University and long-time student of Russian and Soviet affairs. As with the preceding selection, the question arises whether the expectations described can safely be attributed to the main decision makers in the reform, and if so, how important they were relative to other motives.*

Alfred A. Skerpan

Raison d'état:
Economic Expectations

The prevailing economic views respecting serfdom and labor on the eve of reform can be summarized in three propositions: first, labor in bondage meant both an absence of adequate free labor supply and high labor costs and thus was a restraint on a more rapid economic development. Second, a serf population exploited for the private benefit of the landlord was kept impoverished and thus incapable of creating an adequate demand for commerce and the products of machine-age industry. And, third, serf labor, i.e., on corvée, was basically forced labor; and forced labor, denied the enjoyment of its fruits, was unproductive. All of these propositions are finally but applications to Russia of basic lessons from Adam Smith. The extent to which these propositions were true is not of importance in assessing the general motivation of the reformers; they— as many writers then and today, in Russia and out—believed them true. From the propositions flowed the expectations of the economic consequences of freedom. These were: a freely-moving peasantry to serve demands for labor (at lower cost) and the growth of the division of labor, a peasantry availing itself more of its own product and increasing its demand for manufactured goods and other commodities, and, of course, heightened productivity from labor working more for itself. The general end for many of

*From Alfred A. Skerpan, "The Russian National Economy and Emancipation," in Alan D. Ferguson and Alfred Levin (eds.) *Essays in Russian History. A Collection Dedicated to George Vernadsky.* Hamden, Connecticut: Archon Books, 1964, pp. 176–186. Reference notes omitted.

the publicists and reformers was a more powerful state.

The Persistent Role of Government in the Economy

Whatever the expectations were in society after the war, there was little likelihood that the regime would provide society with an effective role in the work of reform. There was no prospect whatsoever that it would summon a national assembly to deal with state finances, such as had been called for by A. I. Koshelev, the slavophile publicist, landowner and entrepreneur. The rule of the autocrat Nicholas had been "not to introduce anything new without regulating what existed and preparing public opinion . . ."; this was to be precisely the rule of his son, even while within the government the need of change for the whole apparatus was recognized. On his deathbed Nicholas expressed regret that he had not been able to do "the good" he wanted, and his last words to Alexander II were: "hold on to everything!"

When the government of Alexander itself embarked on programs to overcome national economic weakness, there was of course no other agency, actual or embryonic, that could proceed to the needed tasks. Nor had the young emperor any intention, with or without his dying father's advice, of permitting a social or political body to rise even as an assisting force. There were, nevertheless, to be moments when this was to seem possible even to him. However, before the process of intervention in the economic scene was completed in this epoch the rising curve of not only civil, but also economic freedom was once more to fall farther below the ascending curve of the power of the state. This was not the product of design; in part it developed even contrary to design. In the end, to use Boris Nolde's hyperbole, even monarchical power had become "a

mere sector of the bureaucratic regime," in which the emperor was but "a kind of supreme functionary."

This dénouement of the "liberation" process, viewed politically, was to be the fruit of the interaction between two tendencies in Russian political "liberalism," one old and one new, with the victory, deceptive as it was, falling to the latter. Socially and emotionally Alexander gravitated toward those who were opposed to this triumph, politically he had little choice but to resist them. With little question, they represented the aristocratic tradition at a time when the condition of state crisis helped recall not only the events of the eighteenth century, but also Decembrism. Very often when "1789" was spoken, as by Alexander to Bismarck, in all probability "1825" lay also in the mind and no doubt closer to the heart.

What aggravated the conflict in Alexander's own person was the circumstance that the aristocrat could speak the catchwords of economic liberalism. This occurred, for example, in final discussions of the State Council over the emancipation statutes. Sharp debate had risen on the provision that two years after the edict the peasants could alter their obligations from corvée to quit-rent without the consent of the landlord. The great majority that opposed it, including all the "feudalists," granted the economic premises; they "recognized that obligatory labor is far from being as productive as the labor of freely hired workers." On this issue, Alexander supported the minority which defended the proposition more positively, but argued as well the benefits to peasants and to the state. In this instance as in an earlier one, where a majority had put itself on the side of the landlord "and society," the minority with Alexander stated its views in terms of the needs of "the development of the industrial forces of the entire state." Of course, much of the conservative—as opposed to reactionary—thought which opposed the government was physiocratic in temper. It not only argued for the well-being of landlord-dominated agriculture, but it stood in sympathy with free trade, or, more accurately, anti-protectionist ideas.

The minority that Alexander found himself supporting represented—apart from possible timeserving—the positions of new-style liberalism. The latter, for our purposes best exemplified in Chicherin's[1] writings, were devoted not only to a mystique of "freedom"; they were also devoted to the mystique of a more comprehensive state power as an instrument to the ultimate social ends. In his *Atenei* memorandum, Chicherin attacked those who defended the old order as a bulwark against the decline of trade, the spread of hunger, and the weakening of the state's authority; this was but an argument in support of "outworn privilege" on the part of those who looked with alarm on government activity in behalf of welfare. What Chicherin and others like him stood for in the economic sphere derived strength from association with old, developing policies of the existing order. It is not at all remarkable that his memorandum, particularly its more specific recommendations, should have influenced some basic procedures in the peasant reform and brought him top level invitations to participate in government work.

Concern with the national economy on the part of the autocratic state was as old as the state itself. Tendencies that can be called mercantilism appeared clearly in the seventeenth century working with tendencies toward political absolutism; and the reign of Peter merely brought them to

fruition. When the ideas of the Enlightenment, through the physiocrats and Adam Smith, challenged mercantilism in respect to the origins of wealth and power, the state, as has been observed, did not hesitate to give serious consideration to them. Indeed, the conviction that complete free trade was necessary for a thriving economy was held from Catherine's time among top servants of the state, notably M. M. Speransky. Partly under the influence of such thinking, Nicholas I also, as has been said, made of commerce, after the army, his second interest. In May, 1833, he tendered a banquet in honor of Russia's entrepreneurs and merchants and showed the deepest interest in Russia's economic growth, even making the prediction that Moscow would become the Russian Manchester.

During his reign special committees were formed in the Ministry of Finance to promote the development of industry and trade. These were served from the 'forties by a policy of a gradual and selective lowering of tariffs; and railroads were promoted for commercial advantage as much as for military reasons. Actually, the Finance Ministry's active concern with manufacturing, in the nineteenth century, ranged back to the time of the Napoleonic wars. Thus, Alexander II's own liberal utterances on economic matters, and his interests in commerce and industry, were not at all isolated from the pattern of thought of his father's reign. His own education, prior to participation in government commissions, had included study in the modern history of England and France and in the political and economic thought associated with it.

Under Nicholas I it was widely accepted too that there was not only a moral case against serfdom, but that there was a strong economic case against it also. More than this, state policy skirted close to lib-

---

[1] B. N. Chicherin (1828–1904): historian, legal scholar, philosopher, and liberal "political man."—Ed.

eration in connection with a series of commissions on the peasant question, even though direct economic considerations apparently played a limited role in their work to the 'forties. However, from 1845 the Minister of Internal Affairs, Count I. A. Perovsky, pointed out some of the economic problems of serfdom, calling it a "mutually unprofitable" relationship and stressing that its abolition was "extremely desirable." Inevitably, there was the parallel political case. Nicholas' chief of gendarmes, Count Benkendorff, in several reports described the social dangers in peasant unrest and called serfdom a powder keg planted under the state, which was "all the more dangerous since the army is made of peasants." All the same, inertia seemed to prevail on the matter of reform.

However, the inertia was only apparent. The work of the commissions, particularly after 1835, in fact established a fundamental policy. By it the peasants on private estates were to be dealt with only after the livelihood and organization of those on the crown lands had been reshaped. These reforms, associated with Count Kiselev in the years 1838–41, not only affected a body of peasants that approximated in number those privately held but served directly as a necessary preliminary and basis for the reform of 1861. Even so, there were those like the ideologue of official nationalism, S. S. Uvarov, the influential Minister of Public Instruction, who could resist final steps as constituting a threat to Russian power. It was also that the economic case against serfdom was not conclusive; economists like Storch and Butovsky and writers like Baron Haxthausen could make a case for its utility in Russia. After serfdom had risen chiefly through indebtedness of the peasantry and then the labor needs of the state, it had continued ultimately because of its overall social and economic utility to the rulers of the country. Had it lacked

this utility, and had it been uneconomic, it obviously would have dissolved of itself long before the mid-nineteenth century, especially in the face of persistent danger. The exploitation, or the privilege of use, of bondage labor was widely accepted as profitable to the very time of emancipation. This will be treated in another context.

Defensible economic worth plus the political uncertainties of a revolutionary age, making undesirable any shocks to the state apparatus, were enough then to sustain the institution for an indeterminable period. In the face of this it would appear that credit is due to Nicholas for what was done. Still more is due when another aspect of the basic problem is recognized. When Count Perovsky[2] urged the need of emancipation, he also urged that it be executed while preserving the position of the landlord and also the security of the state. Given the basic realities of the age this was somewhat visionary. What rendered it impossible was a conviction that was in the 'forties—rather than in the critical year of 1858 as widely believed—already well-rooted in the mind of government. It was held by Perovsky himself and by Nicholas and his Finance Minister; it was a view that was traceable in the thinking of autocracy from 1803. This was that emancipation must not be realized without assuring land for the peasant's use. The position was reflected in two particular decrees.

One of these was the ukase of 1842 which made possible the liberation of peasants with allotment of land in use, in exchange for set obligations; this left the initiative to the landlords and thus was extremely limited in its effect. The year 1846 brought greater disturbances and a fear, for Nicholas, that without stability the "road to communism is ready." After the savage uprising of the peasants in Austrian

---

[2] Minister of Interior, 1846–1852.

Galicia, in February, against the Polish landlords, he responded with the more decisive "Inventory Regulations" the following month. The statute, which actually was the fruit of much longer deliberations, was ultimately applied by fiat to all areas of pre-partition Poland. It directed the giving of lands to the peasants in use and specified both the amount and extent of the obligations to be paid.

The ukase spelled out the reasons for the action, and these with the decree were henceforth continually on the minds of the Russian rulers. While standard histories still ascribe the Galician *jacquerie* to political machinations, the ukase itself went to the bottom of things. In its own words, peasants in the Polish areas showed greater stability where—on lands of the state— they had been freed after 1831, had had their obligations reduced and had their way of life consolidated. In contrast, peasants on the estates of landlords found themselves, it was noted, with obligations undefined in law, and thus subject to the arbitrary acts of their masters, including deprivation of land. The results were, in the words of the ukase: "a pernicious influence on the welfare and morale of the useful class of residents."

Before the outbreak of the Crimean War, then, the stabilizing effects of security in land for the peasant were recognized. Equally clear were the lessons of emancipation in the Germanies and in Austria which neutralized revolutionary tendencies amongst the peasantry. But the problem was how to achieve these goals in Russia while preserving the landowning nobility as a reasonably effective order, on which autocracy was dependent and to which, as it acknowledged, it was firmly attached. The nobles, offered opportunities in 1847 to inaugurate a generous-minded solution, failed expectations. But the following year, the year of revolutions, brought further

proof, particularly in respect to France, of the conservative force of a large propertied peasantry. All the same, the basic problem was not resolved by Nicholas before his death. However, for him probably, as for the peasant, the appearance of a new Napoleon, fighting again on Russian soil, brought its own obvious implications. But it was for his son that the war, with its disastrous external political situation and its accentuation of Russia's economic deficiencies, made the final decisions relatively easy. For serfdom was now at last unequivocally associated with impotence, and freedom of labor was now sharply associated with victory and with heightened national power.

Actually, for Alexander himself the task was not to achieve emancipation but to achieve it with land and preferably with the support of the nobility. Also, from the point of view of economic theory, there would be new problems involved in the association of freedom of labor with freedom with land. These were to muddle the process of liberation and to limit seriously the realization of its prime economic goals. The idea of freedom, however, was the solvent of all doubts. To repeat, what is of significance is that the autocracy now acted mainly to promote greater economic freedom and enterprise as devices to promote greater strength for the state. When the new Minister of the Interior, S. S. Lanskoi, made his first report to Alexander in 1856, before preparations for emancipation had begun, he wrote that "Russian agriculture was far from that degree of development which one could expect." Russia was an agricultural state, he stressed, "and the growth of chiefly its agricultural forces can make possible its prosperity."

Alexander had to tread slowly and cautiously, in good part because the prevailing idea in top government circles, as in society, was that emancipation would but inaugurate a whole pattern of economic and civil reform. His manifesto at the conclusion of peace asked merely that all, equally protected by law, be permitted to enjoy the fruits of their "innocent" labors. And in his remarks to the nobility of Moscow province, made at the end of March, 1856, he asked them "to think about how to bring all this to realization." The nobility, as a body, however, responded at once not to this but to a preceding observation in the same address. This was contained in the famous words, "It is better to begin abolishing serfdom from above than wait until it begins to abolish itself from below." The words were spread widely and burned deep.

More than two years later, and after Alexander had occasion to repeat the observation in the province of Tula, Leo Tolstoi, in an uncirculated and unpublished paper, wrote with fury that it was unjust to accuse the nobles of delay, threatening them with slaughter, "because the Government is weak and inept," and giving them to feel that this would not be a bad thing. "If unfortunately the Government brought us to a liberation from below," Tolstoi wrote further, "and not from above, according to the witty expression of the Lord Emperor, then the least of evils would be the destruction of the government." Much of his feeling stemmed also from the general hostility among the nobles that had been engendered by arbitrary government activity. The mood was such that already in August, 1857, the Secret Committee on peasant matters, whose organization had been Alexander's first procedural step toward reform, could suggest a long drawn-out program without time limit that Alexander accepted. Within three months, however, the final work of emancipation had begun in response to overtures from the nobility of Vilna, Grodno and Kovno provinces.

Economic Expectations in the Reform Process

In the general terminology of the time the term "serfs" was applied primarily to the peasants doing corvée labor for their landlords; they constituted a sizable majority of all landlord held peasants. These were the "enchained work force" cited in the work of one official who utilized an image appearing also in the diary of Leo Tolstoi. Obligatory service meant more than the performance of labor. It meant also a continued subjection to the will, the patrimonial authority of the landlord or his steward, which was far less significant under quit-rent arrangements. The absence of clear-cut definition in law of that authority and the responsibility of the landlord to the state for the peasants' civil obligations, and also for their welfare, were the chief sources of abuse of power and the reduction of such peasants virtually to slavery. For the landlord could, finally, intervene in any phase of the peasant's personal life and could command virtually all his labor, his person and his possessions; for all practical purposes he held over him the powers of life and death.

When on November 20, 1857, Alexander signed the rescript that inaugurated the reform process, it was already clear what ultimate "emancipation" was to mean. First and foremost, it was liberation from the arbitrary authority of the landlord. The rescript called for the preparation by a committee of nobles of a project covering the organization and the "improvement of the way of life" of the peasantry. The quoted phrase, long in use in government circles, may have been but a circumlocution, but it carried a more vital significance than the word "emancipation" might have had. It recurs in official discussions, and, in the final deliberations of the State Council in February, 1861, it was equated with the ending of corvée and was used in fighting off efforts to introduce greater flexibility in the settling of quit rents. Before the end of October, 1858, the immediate objective of a reform law had become, and was to remain to the end, to make "the peasant feel immediately that his life is better." But the next immediate objectives were, recalling Perovsky: to let the "landlord feel immediately assured that his interests were protected" and to establish assurance that "authority would not waver for a moment."

This combination of objectives, as well as the "freedom of labor," was the special challenge of the Editing Commissions that were set up by the Main Committee (of the State Council) at the end of February, 1859, to frame a general project of the final edicts. At the second session the chairman, General Ia. I. Rostovtsov, close associate of the emperor and member of the Committee of Ministers and of the State Council, expressed the leading political expectations: the solution should be such that in it "Russia would for a long time find true security from state disturbance." He himself—with full awareness of Alexander's support—insistently played on the impossibility of maintaining the existing compulsory labor conditions. Where they were necessary in conjunction with the emancipation process, he called for a retention of them only as an "unavoidable *evil*." Once the Commissions started regular work, political considerations were less overt than the economic, and the securing of peasant freedom and way of life was uppermost in the minds of the members. The majority of these, it should be emphasized, were landlords serving as specially invited non-government experts.

The members of the Commissions proceeded under the close guidance of Rostovtsov at the beginning, but also of the representative from the Ministry of Internal Affairs, N. A. Miliutin. But there is little

doubt that for most of them the course of action was much to their way of thinking. They revealed this in their responses to deputies of the provincial nobility, who had framed their own local projects, in accordance with the rescripts and accompanying instructions, and had then been outraged when these were overridden by acts of the government. In August, 1860, Prince V. A. Cherkassky, slavophile-minded private member from the province of Tula, lashed out at the deputies that they, in protesting acts favoring the peasantry, were "now speaking against the Supreme Command, which requires an improvement of the peasants' way of life." To injury he added insult: the landlord was required by law to provide security for his peasants, "but it is nowhere the law that the peasants were bound to provide for the security of him or others."

The panic that some of the deputies showed over the projected loss of corvée labor, and of the land that was to be allotted to the peasants was the panic of landlords who had been actively concerned with agriculture and in the main knew only traditional ways. In the members of the Commissions who, they felt, were responsible for most of the extreme steps being taken, they saw wooly-minded theoreticians who were in fact "socialists" and "communists." To them N. A. Miliutin and P. P. Semenov spoke in terms of the improvements they anticipated from reform: "stimulation of industrial activity in the state [by] the liberation of labor," and a growth of population. Later, Semenov said to another deputy, who also insisted on the importance of corvée labor: "With free labor one can do more . . ., many serf-worker days are [now] expended uselessly. When machines are introduced milling won't be done by hand." And for another deputy, who was afraid that in winter, when there was "snow to the roof," the peasants would ask a thousand rubles to shovel him out, Semenov had again a soothing answer: "Under free labor it will always be possible to find workers . . . [In] winter the peasants do nothing and they will shovel out your home for the lowest pay."

Alexander's own expectations from the final statutes are indicated in the remarks he made to the State Council, as finally approved for the record, in January, 1861. He did not omit references to the political consequences of any delay in approving the final statutes, in fact he suggested possible dire consequences for the state and the landlords and he referred once more to his famed statement in Moscow in 1856. However, before this and at the end appeared the overriding concern. On liberation would depend for Russia, he said, "the growth of its forces and power." In a final prayer he called for God's blessing to end the business at hand "for the future prosperity of our beloved Fatherland." The manifesto, signed February 19 and proclaimed from Sunday, March 5, 1861, carried as its first specific reference one to freedom. The phrase, unfortunately, lacked the impact it should have had: "the enserfed people will receive in proper time full rights of rural residents."

The peasants, unlike the gentry landowners, were not consulted by the state in its preparation of the reform. Crucial evidence on peasant attitudes toward the emancipation was nevertheless provided by the extensive disorders that broke out almost immediately following publication of the emancipation manifesto. The author of many works on European intellectual history from the Enlightenment to the twentieth century, FRANCO VENTURI (b. 1914), professor of modern history at the University of Turin, has devoted a chapter of his monumental history of Russian Populism to the peasant movement of the early 1860s. Of particular interest in this account is his attempt to reconstruct the peasants' idea of "real emancipation." Given the marked contrast between these expectations and the promulgated reform, which he holds responsible for the extensive disorders of 1861–1862, how does Venturi explain the rapid decline in the number of disorders following 1862?*

Franco Venturi

The Peasant Movement

As soon as Alexander II came to the throne, insistent rumours of an immediate emancipation spread throughout the countryside. Official statistics speak of twenty-five upheavals in 1856, of forty in 1857, and it must be remembered that only the most serious cases were recorded. But more important than numbers (never very accurate) is the character of the more influential movements. In 1856 entire villages of southern Russia were set in motion by a rumour that free land was being distributed in those parts of the Crimea which had been devastated by the war. In the departments of Ekaterinoslav and of Kherson, for example, there was a persis-tent rumour that "the Tsar was in the isthmus of Perekop with a helmet of gold and was granting freedom to all who came there, whereas those who did not come or who arrived late would remain serfs of the landlords as before." "Influenced by these rumours," reports I. I. Ignatovich, "the peasants moved with their families and all their goods, sometimes in entire villages, in search of the legendary Tsar, hoping to become free colonizers in the Crimea." In the vast majority of cases they took leave of the landowners in the most friendly manner, though they seized the cattle they needed and their working tools. Sometimes they went to the landlord to say farewell

*From *Roots of Revolution*, by Franco Venturi. © Copyright 1960 by George Weidenfeld and Nicholson, Ltd. Reprinted by permission of Alfred A. Knopf, Inc. Pp. 206–219.

and to thank him for his care of them. Only in one case, in the department of Ekaterinoslav, was their departure marked by disorders. "As the peasants left they flung themselves on to the landlord's house and began to loot everything that came to hand, rejoicing that they had killed a steward and threatening the landlord himself. Eventually they took all their goods and their cattle, and after destroying the doors and windows of the house they went off." [1] Nine thousand peasants set off from the region of Ekaterinoslav, three thousand from Kherson, and many from surrounding districts. Troops had to intervene; there were ten dead, and many wounded.

Meanwhile disturbances increased and spread throughout the Empire. In the first four months of 1858 alone, seventy cases of collective acts of insubordination were recorded, and by the end of the year there were over two hundred. But it is unlikely that the movements had been resumed on a large scale. The very high figure is probably due to the fact that in the decisive period of drawing up the reforms, the central authorities wanted more detailed news, and local officials therefore reported events which in previous years they would not have mentioned. So the unrest continued, spreading throughout all the departments, but without assuming alarming proportions. A report spoke of seventy cases in 1859 and of a hundred in 1860. Impatience for freedom was intense; news from the provinces drew attention to the urgent need to solve the problem of serfdom, but no new facts succeeded in modifying the Emperor's decisions and the despatch of the various Commissions.

The explicit promise of emancipation had had a profound effect on the peasants.

It was no longer a question of changing a few details in their relations with the landlords. They now expected complete emancipation. Nicholas I's cautious measures had produced a strong reaction. Alexander II's promises made the peasants think of their own interests, and draw up immediate demands to defend their work and their bread. The most obvious development that can be detected in the villages immediately before 19th February 1861 consists in a passive resistance to the corvées. The peasants carried out these duties, from which they thought they would soon be exempted, more and more slowly and more and more reluctantly. A sort of spontaneous strike, aimed at loosening the bonds of serfdom, and making submission to the local administrative authorities less specific, accompanied, and often partly replaced an open but sporadic refusal to yield to the landlord's will. All this, of course, only took place within the limits possible in a social régime which for the moment was still intact and which still showed itself able to enforce severe repressive measures. There were too some signs of doubt and distrust. "It would have been better if the Emperor had not promised us freedom, as he is not in a position to control the landowners," the peasants were saying at the end of 1859. These signs of disappointment were all the more frequent in that the landowners were looking to their immediate interests; they often profited from the respite allowed by the slow processes of the law to seize the peasants' land and in general to make as much use of their serfs as they could. But soon the peasants began to hope again. Anyone coming to the village was thought to be the messenger of "freedom." Once again it began to be whispered that the edict was already in existence but that the landowners and the authorities were keeping it hidden. In market places excited discussions

[1] I. I. Ignatovich, 'Osnovnyye cherty krest'yanskikh volneniy pered osvobozhdeniem' (The fundamental nature of the peasant disorders which preceded the liberation), op. cit., p. 207.

among the peasants on their future became frequent.

The publication of the manifesto on 19th February brought back in a flash all the hopes, and disappointments, of the peasants. Throughout 1861 the great news of freedom produced a state of passionate excitement. The peasants protested against any aspect of the new situation which did not correspond to their immediate interests or to the notion of freedom that they had already formed. Then in the two following years hopes began to wane; the wave of excitement ebbed. The blow was severe and it left indelible traces on the most sensitive men of all classes. But it did not lead to a political upheaval. The situation which seemed so revolutionary did not end in revolution.[2]

Between 1861 and 1863 eleven hundred cases of disorder, large and small, were reported. Some of them were of considerable size, and though they did not seriously endanger the safety of the State, they showed how bitter was the discontent seething in the masses. From the documents that I have seen it is not possible to classify exactly these disturbances during the three years that followed the emancipation. I. I. Ignatovich has examined three hundred and eighteen cases and concludes that they can be divided in chronological order as follows:

1861	279
1862	35
1863	4

The dates of the remaining cases are not certain. Other documents confirm that this was the general trend of the upheavals which were particularly violent in the summer following the manifesto and then rapidly diminished.

Some of the disorders at least were due to technical errors involved in the publication of the "Emancipation." The manifesto and legislative arrangements were drawn up in a complicated, vague and rhetorical style, which seemed calculated to lead to doubts and false interpretation. The Russian administration spent a generation trying to clarify the contradictions in the document and the various circulars which followed. The uncertainty of the peasants in 1861 can easily be imagined. They were almost all unable to read, and were totally incapable of understanding the public reading of such remarkably obscure pronouncements. The documents were not even translated into the different national languages of the various populations who did not speak Russian. The number of copies circulated to local authorities was inadequate. Here and there local governments reprinted them, but this helped to spread the rumour that other manifestos were in existence more favourably disposed to the peasants and had been hidden by the cunning of the authorities.

These technical errors clearly reflected the political and social position of Russia

---

[2] Of the extensive documentation on the subject, consisting generally of local and of detailed studies, the principal works are: I. I. Ignatovich. '*Volneniya pomeshchich'ikh krest'yan ot 1854 do 1863 goda*' (*The risings of peasants who belonged to landlords, from 1854-1863*), in 'Minuvshiye gody,' 1908, nos. VII–XI; A. Popel'nitsky, '*Kak prinyato bylo polozhenie 19 fevralya 1861 g. osvobozhdyonnymi krest'yanami*' (*How the freed peasants received the manifesto of 19th February 1861*), in 'Sovremennyy mir,' 1911, nos. II–III; P. A. Zayonchkovsky, '*Provedenie v zhizn' krest'yanskoy reformy 1861 g.*' (*The enforcement of the peasant reform of 1861*), M., 1958. The most important publications of documents relating to this subject are: '*Krest'yanskoye dvizhenie v 1861 godu posle otmeny krepostnogo prava*. Podgotovil k pechati E. A. Morokhovets (*The peasant movement in 1861, after the abolition of serfdom*. Edited for publication by E. A. Morokhovets), M.-L., 1949; and '*Otmena krepostnogo prava. Doklady ministrov vnutrennykh del o provedenii krest'-yanskoy reformy 1861-1862*' (*The abolition of serfdom. Reports of Ministers of the Interior on the application of peasant reforms, 1861-1862*), edited by S. N. Valk, M.-L., 1950. On all this period, see the collective work, '*Velikaya reforma*' (*The great reform*), by A. K. Dzhivilegov, S. P. Mel'gunov and B. I. Picheta, M., 1911.

at this time. The muddled style of the decrees mirrored the uncertainty and fears of the ruling classes, which resulted from the compromise so laboriously arranged between the nobility, the bureaucracy and the Emperor. The very difficulties met with in making the edict known showed how great was the lack of any organic connecting body between the State and the great mass of serfs.

The clergy was instructed to read the manifesto from the pulpit, but the village priests were usually so uneducated that they were not even able to do this correctly. Their lack of preparation became all too apparent when during the following months the peasants came to seek further explanations and clarification. In some cases it is obvious that the priests were so close to the peasants both in mentality and interests that they interpreted these peasants' hopes and demands further than the manifesto and were far from being a force on which the government could rely to carry out its reforms.

The case of the clergy was only one of the symptoms of the administrative crisis in the Russian village of 1861. The gentry (pomeshchiki) had been the pivot of the ancien régime, and Nicholas I well knew that they were the foundations of his empire. This was a dangerous situation which tended to transform any economic struggle between serf and landlord into a revolt against the State. The period of the great reform started when cases of insubordination became more frequent and when it was obvious that the state of mind of the peasants towards their owners was changing. The moment had come to create different relations between the State and the village.

The year 1861 was a time of transition. The nobles had lost their powers but the new local bureaucracy had not yet taken root and the peasant communities had not been brought under the control of the ad-ministration. To fill the gap recourse was had to the army, to floggings and repression; and this naturally only embittered the conflict. But meanwhile a new machinery of government was being created. "Arbitrators" were elected to decide on the relations between the peasants and the landlords, and to determine the size of land granted to the obshchina and the amount of the redemption fee. Village administration was reformed, with representatives elected by the inhabitants and controlled by the State bureaucracy. And finally in 1864 the Zemstvo took provincial life in hand and created a new basis of collaboration between the nobles and the other classes.

As had occurred while the reforms were being prepared, these changes, willed from above, could only be put into effect through the cooperation of those who were in varying degrees impregnated with the spirit of the intelligentsia. It was men of this kind who were elected "arbitrators" and who restored to the peasants a minimum of faith in the justice of the ruling classes and the State. It was they who created in the Zemstvo a local ruling class which was sufficiently enlightened to appreciate the economic changes which were occurring in the village and to bring some education and help, the lack of which had been so painfully felt in 1861. From the point of view of the revolutionaries and the Populists the final result of the reforms was to "surround the life of the people with a complete amphitheatre of regulations, each one of which could obstruct the fair development of the people's life. The exclusively noble administration of the time of the serfs has been replaced by an administration made up of officials and gentry," said N. A. Serno-Solovevich, the founder of Zemlya i Volya.[3] But this was

---

[3] N. A. Serno-Solov'evich, 'Okonchatel'noye reshenie krest'yanskogo voprosa' (The final solution of the peasant problem), Berlin, 1861, p. 64.

the only way to restrain and halt the peasant outburst of 1861. It also explains the rapid decline in the number of disorders in the following two years.

Despite this the movement of 1861 had had time to express at least in outline what the peasants expected of an emancipation really corresponding to their ideals and interests. As a rule their protests were not directed against specific details of the new legislation but against its very spirit. I. I. Ignatovich has classified 325 of these disorders as follows:

1. Protests against the
   manifesto as a whole   1861   192
      1862   26
      1863   2

2. Protests against particular
   items   1861   43
      1862   None
      1863   None

3. Protests against abuses of
   the authorities   1861   9
      1862   6
      1863   None

4. Unknown reasons   1861   41
      1862   4
      1863   2

Despite the fact that the three hundred and twenty-five cases here examined are probably the most serious, and that the importance of protests against the manifesto as a whole would probably be less significant if all the risings of 1861 were taken into account, these figures do show the general tendency.

Disorders provoked by the contrasts between "liberty of the people" *(volya narodnaya)* and "freedom of the State" *(volya kazennaya)* were particularly severe. Emancipation, it was thought, would mean the complete abolition of existing obligations: no more *corvées,* no more taxes either in kind or in cash; the village would govern itself in accordance with its age-old traditions and customs.

Sometimes the peasants expressed this belief by their desire to belong to the Tsar, to the State, i.e. to move into a better economic situation and escape the direct impact of the owner's authority. In a village in the Vladimir district the peasants interpreted the manifesto as an order by the Tsar to grant them land from the property belonging to the State. "And they swore together that they would pay nothing more to the landlord." [4] In 1862 the peasants of the village of Pustoboytov (Poltava) claimed that "they and their land were free." If the Tsar had freed them, it meant that they were his peasants and no longer the squire's.[5]

But as a rule their demands were not based on the contrast between their position and that of the State peasants. They made it increasingly plain that they wanted a freedom which would entirely exempt them from any obligation to the gentry or administration. In April a crowd of a thousand peasants assembled in a village in the department of Voronezh and replied to the authorities that "the Tsar had sent them a most merciful edict, that they were now free and that they no longer intended to pay their *redevances* or carry out their duties on the landlords' property." When the Governor explained to them that this was not the case, they began to fling their caps in the air and shout: "We no longer want the landlord. Down with the landlord! We have already worked enough! Now is the time for freedom!" "These ideas," commented the writer of the report from which these words are quoted, "spring from almost

---

[4] 'Krest'yanskoye dvizhenie v 1861 godu' (The peasant movement in 1861), *op. cit.,* pp. 35-6.

[5] I. I. Ignatovich, 'Volneniya pomeshchich'ikh krest'yan' (The risings of peasants who belonged to landlords), *op. cit.,* no. VIII.

three centuries of serfdom and cannot be cancelled at a blow." The movement spread to surrounding villages and was suppressed only by sending troops. The "instigators" were arrested, but the leading one was able to escape. Alexander II noted on the margin of the report: "Thank God it's ended like this." [6]

In the region of Kursk too it was obvious what the peasants felt. "They are extremely suspicious both of the landlord and of the rural police." [7] There, too, disorders arose because of their desire to free themselves from both these authorities. In the department of Minsk, risings spread to the shout of: "Hold fast. Our turn has come." The peasants were convinced that the Tsar had given them "freedom and the land" (*volya i zemlya*).[8] In the village of Kadymkor (in the department of Perm) the peasants said that the manifesto which had been read out by the local policeman was a fake, as the real one must of course be written in letters of gold. Two thousand of them assembled to demand an explanation for "a kind of liberty that leaves us just as before under the authority of the Count our landlord." They gave in only after two had been killed and eight wounded.[9]

Further examples of such protests could easily be given. The revolt, whether open or concealed, against all local authorities, turned everyone's attention to the distant power that had done away with serfdom— the Tsar. The marshal of the aristocracy in the province of Podolsk gave a vivid description of this state of mind in a report of August 1861:

The Tsar has taken on in their eyes a sort of abstract significance, completely distinct from any executive authority, which, they think, has been sold to the nobility. This sort of idea re-

garding the supreme power is certainly not new in the history of the masses, but it is always dangerous because it ends by attributing to the supreme power aims which it has never had, and by reducing all executive orders of the State to impotence. The peasants expect everything to come direct from the Tsar, to whom they give the character of a natural force, blind and implacable. They have completely given up believing in the simplest rules of respect for the property of others and for the general economic rules which are laid down in the manifesto of 19th February ... What they have been granted appears not to correspond to the size of the transformation which they had expected; and so they refuse to believe what is written. According to them, because for once fate has turned the natural force of supreme power to their advantage, they now have the right to expect from it every kind of benefit and generosity ...[10]

The peasants made frequent attempts to get into contact with a Tsar who was at once omnipotent and simultaneously unable to make his voice felt in their miserable villages. They sent messengers who were of course arrested. They always invoked the Tsar in their clashes with the local authorities, and here and there they ended by believing people who said that they had been sent by the Tsar or members of the imperial family. "In March 1861 a soldier from the department of Samara, travelling through villages on the Crown lands, passed himself off as Prince Constantine Nikolaevich or the Emperor himself ... telling the peasants that they too would soon have their freedom." [11] In the summer of 1862 two "usurpers" went round villages in the department of Perm "to see how the gentry were behaving to-

---

[6] *'Krest'yanskoye dvizhenie v 1861 godu'* (*The peasant movement in 1861*), *op. cit.*, p. 46.

[7] *Ibid.*, p. 117.

[8] *Ibid.*, p. 116.

[9] *'Kolokol,'* 1862, no. 134.

[10] *'Krest'yanskoye dvizhenie v 1861 godu'* (*The peasant movement in 1861*), *op. cit.*, p. 174.

[11] The annual report of the Third Section published in *'Krest'yanskoye dvizhenie, 1827-1869.'* Podgotovil k pechati E. A. Morokhovets (*The peasant movement, 1827-1869*. Edited for publication by E. A. Morokhovets), M.-L, 1931, vol. II, p. 3.

wards their peasants, and to investigate whether they had given a false interpretation of the decree of emancipation," which they said contained a promise of complete exemption from all dues. Troops had to be used to suppress the disturbances which they aroused. The peasants were also convinced that they were to receive not only land but cattle directly from the Tsar.[12]

But these were only sporadic cases. The conviction that the Tsar had granted the peasants "true liberty" was so widespread that it was not even felt necessary to obtain confirmation by getting into contact with him: it was enough to read the manifesto correctly. It was, of course, easy enough to discover men ready to find in the law just what was wanted, all the more so as the peasants were prepared to pay those able to read the necessary documents. Ex-soldiers, scribes, the odd Pole or Jew in the western territories, priests, bigots of the *Raskol*, all became interpreters of the great hopes which were coursing through the villages and provided the immediate cause of most of the disturbances.

Two districts in the region of Penza, for example, were deeply stirred by the "interpretation" given by a seventy-year-old soldier, Andrey Semenov Elizarov, who had fought against Napoleon and had been to Paris in 1814. He enjoyed great influence over his fellow peasants whom he made call him "Count Tolstoy." In April 1861, dressed in his old soldier's uniform and wearing all his medals, he persuaded them "to fight for God and the Tsar." Twenty-six villages refused to go on obeying their landlords and the authorities. A crowd of three hundred peasants flung themselves on the first troops who were sent to disperse them. After a clash in which the peasants lost three dead and four wounded, but also succeeded in taking

two prisoners (including a non-commissioned officer), the troops had to withdraw. The movement spread. The news reached Penza that "ten thousand peasants had rallied to the cry of 'Freedom! Freedom!' *(Volya! Volya!)*, and were carrying a red flag through the villages, insulting clergymen, beating up the rural authorities and threatening to do the same with the administrative and military leaders, and declaring that the 'land is all ours. We do not want to pay the *obrok* [dues] and we will not work for the landlords.' " When the troops again advanced the peasants said that they were "ready to die for God and for the Tsar," and that they refused "to work for the landlords" even if they were hanged for it, but "would rather that the last one of them should die." They held fast in a series of clashes. Two salvoes failed to disperse the crowd. "We will die but we will not give in," they said. Standing at the head of the peasants, Elizarov shouted to the General in charge of operations, "We must all support the cause of justice. Why deceive you?" Only after eight dead and twenty-seven wounded had been left on the field and the more determined peasants had been taken prisoner, tried on the spot and flogged, did the disturbance gradually quieten down. Elizarov and another "instigator" were taken prisoner and exiled to the region of Irkutsk in Siberia.[13]

Another mouthpiece of the peasants' aspirations made his appearance in this rising. Of Leonty Egortsev, an official report said:

He belonged to the sect of the Molokane (milk-drinkers) and he soon succeeded in gaining a great influence over the entire territory. His false interpretations and the special powers of which he boasted inspired such great faith that villages sent him troikas imploring him to

---

[12] I. I. Ignatovich, 'Volneniya pomeshchich'ikh krest'yan' (The risings of peasants who belonged to landlords), op. cit., no. VIII.

[13] 'Krest'yanskoye dvizhenie v 1861 godu' (The peasant movement in 1861), op. cit., pp. 142 ff.

come and explain to them the manifesto. They took him by the arm and carried a small bench behind him, made him climb on to it, and so he proclaimed liberty for everyone. So great did his powers become that he even began to collect money and to threaten to hang anyone who disobeyed him as well as those responsible for the repression.

By his threats he convinced the peasants that "no one even if threatened with death should denounce his own comrades," and that they should pay no attention either to the rural police or to the representatives of the nobility or even to the General in command of the local troops whom he called "the Tsar's Ambassador" and who had been "bought by the gentry." He also went through the villages saying: "If the troops fire on you, hold fast for three salvoes and then the authorities themselves will give you true freedom."

It was sectarian preaching of this kind that led to the most serious disturbances of 1861—those of Bezdna.[14]

The region of Spassk between the Volga and the Kama contained twenty-three thousand souls (heads of families). It was not a poor district. General Apraksin, who was responsible for suppressing the revolt, said that its peasants were "very prosperous." Although the great majority were of Russian origin, there were also, as throughout the department of Kazan, some Tartar colonies.

When the manifesto was published, the inhabitants began to look around for some-

one who would interpret it in line with their ambitions. Eventually a peasant from the village of Bezdna, by dint of examining the text succeeded in finding what he was looking for. Anton Petrov was a *raskolnik*.[15] He was able to read and had the typical sectarian veneration for the written word, believing that the printed text *must* contain truth as long as one could succeed in reading it. The mere sight of two noughts [00] used instead of a blank space to indicate a figure which had not yet been decided was enough to convince him that the freedom was "false." True liberty would have had the Cross of St Anne, which he recognized in a "10%" printed in another part of the statute. From then on Petrov began to preach his variety of "liberty." Serfdom had long been abolished, but the authorities were concealing this from the peasants. They must now be made to read out the authentic text.

He was thought to be a prophet. The peasants rushed to him, not just from the neighbouring villages, but from the surrounding provinces of Samara and Simbirsk. He began to acquire real power over the peasants belonging both to the landlords and the State, over Russians and Tartars.

I told all who came to me that the peasants were free. I told them not to obey the gentry and the authorities. I ordered them not to work the *corvées;* not to pay the *obrok;* and not to do anything when they saw others taking wheat from the landlords' stores. If the water was ruining the mill, it was not up to them to help repair it. I explained that all the land belonged to them and that the gentry would keep only a third of it. I invented all this out of my own head, so as to attract the peasants from my district, assuming that the more of them there were, the sooner they would succeed in obtaining freedom. Many came to me, and I declared them free. To win over still more, I suggested

---

[14] I. I. Ignatovich, 'Bezdna,' in *'Velikaya reforma,' op. cit.,* vol., V, pp. 211 ff.; M. Nechkina, *'Vosstanie v Bezdne' (The insurrection in Bezdna),* in 'Krasnyy Arkhiv', 1929, no. IV; M. Nechkina, *'Iz istorii krest'yanskikh vosstaniy protiv "voli"' (From the history of peasant insurrections against the 'liberation'),* ibid., 1929, no. V; E. I. Ustyuzhanin, *'Bezdnenskoye vosstanie 1861 g.' (The insurrection at Bezdna in 1861),* in *'Uchyennyye zapiski Kazanskogo Pedagogicheskogo Instituta,'* 1941, no. IV; and *'Bezdenskoye vosstanie 1861 g.'* Sbornik dokumentov. Obshchaya redaktsiya A. I. Yampol'skoy i D. S. Gutmana *(The insurrection at Bezdna in 1861.* Collected documents, under the general editorship of A. I. Yampol'skaya and D. S. Gutman), Kazan, 1948.

---

[15] Schismatic, unreformed Orthodox "old believer."—Ed.

that the *mir* should elect new administrators, whom I sent to other villages to prepare the peasants to receive their freedom.

In many villages new administrators were elected, and they began to demand account books from the local authorities to keep a check on their activities. The peasant communities met together in assemblies and began by deciding on collective abstention from all work on the landlords' properties. At Bezdna and other centres the police were driven away, for, said the peasants, the authorities were lying, and the Tsar had ordered them not to spare the nobles but to cut off their heads.

Gradually a real organization began to take shape, based on Anton Petrov's *izba*[16] at Bezdna. Every kind of rumour began to spread. Constantine Nikolaevich was in prison at Bezdna, and asked the peasants to come and free him. Another prince, Nikolay Pavlovich, had been killed by the gentry. News of true freedom would soon arrive. There was no need to be frightened by the soldiers; even if they did shoot, it was only necessary to hold fast; at the third salvo the authorities themselves would proclaim true liberty.

Anton Petrov continued to preach. One of his speeches has been reported as follows:

You will have true liberty only if you defend the man who finds it for you. Much peasant blood will be spilt before it is finally proclaimed. But the Tsar has given definite orders that you must mount a guard round that man day and night, on foot and on horseback; that you must defend him from all attacks; and not allow either the landlords or the clergy or the officials to reach him; that you must not hand him over, and not remove him from his *izba*. If they burn down one side of the village, do not abandon the *izba*; if they burn down the other side, do not abandon the *izba*. Young men and old will come to you; do not let them reach me; do not hand me over to them. They will cheat

you by saying that they have come from the Tsar; do not believe them. The old men will come with smiles; middle-aged men will come; both bald and hairy men will come; and every kind of official; but you must not hand me over. And in due time, a young man will come here sent by the Tsar. He will be seventeen years old, and on his right shoulder he will have a gold medal and on his left shoulder a silver one. Believe him, and hand me over to him. They will threaten you with soldiers, but do not be afraid; no one will dare to beat the Russian, Christian people without orders from the Tsar. And if the nobles buy them, and they fire at you, then destroy with your axes these rebels against the will of the Tsar.

On the night of 11th April, the roads leading to Bezdna were full of peasants on horseback and on foot, all making for the *izba* of Anton Petrov "who gave freedom and land; who appointed new authorities and said that he would soon give freedom to thirty-four departments."

On the following morning, General Apraksin arrived at the head of two hundred and thirty soldiers. At the entrance of the village he saw a table with bread and salt on it, and two old men without hats. He asked them: "Whom have you prepared all this for?" Doubtfully they answered: "For you, on the orders of the authorities" (i.e. those elected by the rebels). "I later learnt that this welcome had been prepared for those who came to announce their support for Anton Petrov."

Facing us at the end of the road, round Petrov's house, was a dense mass of five thousand people. I halted the troops and went forward to about a hundred and eighty paces from them. I then sent on ahead two of the Governor's adjutants to give a first warning to the peasants. But their words were drowned by shouts of "Freedom! Freedom!" They came back, warning the peasants that if they did not hand over Anton Petrov and if they did not disperse, they would be fired at. I then sent on a priest who held up a cross and called upon them for a long time, saying that if they did not surrender and

---

[16] A peasant dwelling.—Ed.

return to their houses they would be fired at. They went on shouting. Then I myself went forward and explained my orders and commanded them to hand over Anton Petrov and to go away. But this had no effect on their terrible obstinacy. They shouted: "We do not need an envoy from the Tsar. Give us the Tsar himself. Fire on us, but you will not be firing on us but on Alexander Nikolaevich." I forced them to keep silence and said, "I am sorry for you, my lads, but I must fire and I will fire. Those who feel themselves innocent move off." But I saw that no one moved and that the crowd continued to shout and to resist. So I turned back and ordered one of the ranks to fire one salvo. I then gave them another warning. But the crowd went on shouting. I was then compelled to order a few salvoes. I was forced to do this mainly because the peasants, noting the considerable gap between the salvoes, began to come out from their houses in large numbers shouting to each other to dig up posts and threatening to surround and submerge my small company. Eventually the crowd dispersed and shouts were heard offering to hand over Anton Petrov. He meanwhile tried to flee into an orchard at the back of his house which had been held in readiness for the occasion. Then he came out of the house and went towards the soldiers, carrying the manifesto of emancipation on his head. There he was taken, together with his accomplices, and led under escort to the prison of Spassk. After Petrov's surrender, the corpses were carried off and a search made for the wounded. After confirmation it appeared that there were fifty-one dead and seventy-seven wounded.

From another source we learn that Anton Petrov was "thirty-five years old; thin, small and white as a sheet, and terribly frightened at the thought that he would be immediately shot." In fact his spirits remained high even in prison and during the investigations.

When the troops reached our village, I was in the *izba* . . . When the first and second salvoes of guns were fired, I prayed and said nothing. After the third I said to the peasants, "Do not surrender, lads; it's not time yet. Now

they will stop firing and read out the manifesto of freedom." I said these words so as to hold firm for freedom to the very end. At the fourth salvo I wanted to go away, but while my parents were giving me their blessing, other salvoes were fired. After I had said farewell to my parents, I took the manifesto on my head and went towards the soldiers, thinking that with the Tsar's *ukaz* on my head, they would not fire at me. I did not want to run away . . .

After a quick trial, a military tribunal condemned him to death. His sentence said among other things that the rising he had provoked "had threatened the entire department of Kazan." He was shot on 19th April.

Even before he had been executed, the legends began to spread. It was said that he had been clothed in a cloak of gold, given a sword and sent to the Tsar himself by General Apraksin. He would soon return with freedom. After his death it was said that he was a martyr, that a fire had sprung up on his tomb and an angel dressed in white had announced that he would soon be resurrected. As General Apraksin said in a report of 14th May, the requiem ceremony at Kazan, organized by the students of the university and the Ecclesiastical Academy, including Shchapov,[17] helped to convince the peasants that Anton Petrov was a prophet.

An enormous impression was made by the rising and massacre at Bezdna. The nobles of Kazan spoke of "a new Pugachev" and put pressure on the authorities to take stronger steps. More troops were stationed in the district of Spassk. Among the intellectuals the salvoes fired at Bezdna aroused varying reactions of reverence, surprise or fear, and helped to deepen growing internal dissensions. In London Herzen was able to give the readers of the *Kolokol* a remarkably full and detailed account of what had happened in that re-

[17] A. P. Shchapov (1830–1876): historian of religious sectarianism, professor at Kazan University.—Ed.

mote corner of the Kazan region. The first news and then Apraksin's reports merely confirmed the exiles' theory that the manifesto of 19th February had imposed a new serfdom on Russia.[18]

Disturbances aimed at finding or applying "true freedom" continued throughout 1862 and 1863, though on a reduced scale. In the department of Saratov, for example, two villages, Klyuchy and Stary Chirigin, refused to come to any agreement with the landlord to work the land assigned to them, saying that "Satan had built his house among them, stopped them living, and had put a curse on them." They called the gentry and officials "gypsies and mad dogs come to drink their blood." Two peasant delegates were arrested and then freed because of pressure from their compatriots. The repression was violent and cruel. Women with children at their breasts threw themselves on the soldiers, asking to be flogged in place of their menfolk.[19]

But as time passed the peasants had to concede that the manifesto was in fact the Tsar's law. Their aspirations to "true liberty" were postponed to the distant future. The decree itself allowed for a transitional period of two years during which the peasants would remain as "peasants with limited obligations." Once the peasants' new legal status had been brought into being and the estates had been divided between landlord and community, feudal ties would lapse and the *corvées* would be abolished. Only economic ties would remain between the landed estate and the village. These would be based on the redemption fee, on the renting of the landlords' property and on the use of paid labour. The peasant "interpreters" repeated

this and claimed that the peasants would remain serfs until 19th February 1863. On that day the Tsar would grant a second, the real, freedom. And so they drew the logical conclusion that during those two years of delay it was essential not to sign any contract or agreement. They were frightened of committing themselves too soon, and running the risk that their hands would be tied when their land and freedom became due. Far better, they thought, to continue working in the *corvées* and paying feudal obligations as before. Nothing must be done until the great day.

This idea had gained currency during the last days of the Bezdna rising. "Brothers, let us wait for the second freedom instead of this wretched one that they have granted us," said the peasants after the repression. Many communities were encouraged by this to refuse to make the agreements envisaged by the law, even when they were in their own interests. The "arbitrators" often met this additional obstacle in the course of their duties.

In July 1862, the entire village of Olshansk in the region of Kursk was convinced that "if anyone works the land granted to him before the end of two years, he will remain a serf forever. On the other hand, those who refuse to work the land granted to them, will be free." A squadron of Hussars was sent and frightened the peasants, but met with strong resistance when trying to make arrests. A bayonet charge was made, and the peasants fled to the woods and for long refused to surrender.[20] The same sort of resistance, though in different forms, occurred elsewhere. In 1861 eight cases of unrest were recorded, all inspired by the idea of "a new freedom." In 1862 there were twenty-one, and another two during the first month of 1863. Hope seemed to grow as 19th February drew near. Finally the Emperor

---

[18] 'Kolokol,' nos. 98–9, 100, 101, 122–3, 124 and 125.

[19] I. I. Ignatovich, '*Volneniya pomeshchich'ikh krest'yan*' (*The risings of peasants who belonged to landlords*), *op. cit.*, no. IX.

[20] *Ibid, op. cit.*, no. X.

himself thought it advisable to make a public denial of any impending new freedom.

We have now reached the final date of the great peasant movement, and can try to look at it as a whole and grasp its essential characteristics.

Only in extreme cases had the peasants demanded *all* the land, including the landlords' property. Even Anton Petrov thought that the gentry should be allowed to retain a third of their estates. The cry "All the land is ours" was heard here and there in 1861, but it implied a principle rather than an immediate demand. The landowners' houses were not touched and no attempt was made to seize their estates though the peasants refused to farm them.

What the peasants meant by their dreams of "true liberty" was mainly the complete separation of their community from the landlord, the breaking of all ties between them and hence the *obshchina* closing in on itself. If they imagined that the Tsar's "second liberty" was going to grant them the land, it was because they hoped to receive it free, without having to pay the redemption fee, and without having to remain economically and morally bound to the landlord. If they refused so often to make the agreements provided for by the law, it was because they thought that by so doing they were avoiding new taxes which were being imposed on them. The decree of liberation itself allowed for the granting of a reduced strip of land (a quarter of the normal) to anyone not able to pay the redemption fee. The peasants often submitted to this expedient, which was quite insufficient to keep them alive, so as to avoid tying their hands for the future, and falling back into a condition indistinguishable from the serfdom they had suffered for centuries.

But the most violent demonstrations and revolts were not directed against the re-demption fee. This was still in the future, too vague and too remote to be seriously alarming. It was only very rarely that the peasants were themselves making the demands that Chernyshevsky was at this time making on their behalf—that the fee should be contributed to by the whole country and not merely by the peasants. Only once do we find among the documents of 1861 the idea of "the Tsar's redemption," a primitive expression of the idea that the State should compensate the landowners.[21]

Their ambitions were more immediate, and were concerned with the abolition of the *corvées* and other obligations. In other words, they merely expressed with greater violence what they had already made clear before the reform: their refusal to farm the landlords' property for nothing. At first they had confined themselves to a slow and prolonged strike, now they sometimes tried direct refusal. But the law itself provided for these changes, and even the landowners hastened its application, for they were convinced that with the decline in their power and authority it was no longer possible to retain the *corvée*. The revolts and the rebellious state of mind of the peasants, whether open or suppressed, only hastened a process which was latent in events themselves.

From the administrative point of view too, the disturbances of these years had brought to light the peasants' ambition to run their own communities by themselves. Some of the elections provided for by legal decree had to be carried out at the point of the bayonet, in face of a crowd of peasants obstinately insisting on their right to change their leaders when and how they

---

[21] The peasants of the village of Karasin in Volhynia began a revolt in 1862 which they kept up until 1867; they refused to come to terms, saying 'we will wait for the Tsar's redemption.' Ignatovich, *op. cit.*, no. VIII.

wanted. In the Bezdna rising, for instance, a number of villages, as we have seen, began to create their own administrations and drive out all representatives of the State bureaucracy.

Such symptoms were important in revealing the determination of the villages to live their own lives. But they were only the most obvious aspects of that desire for isolation which inspired the entire peasant class and which led them to face the army's rifles unarmed and impassive, and to "die for God and the Tsar" while waiting for a mythical "second freedom."

One of the most productive and wide-ranging Soviet specialists in modern Russian history is P. A. ZAIONCHKOVSKII (b. 1904), professor of history at Moscow University. The outstanding contemporary authority on emancipation of the serfs, he is the author of a major contribution to the field entitled *The Implementation of the Peasant Reform of 1861* (1958) and a standard general study of the reform, *The Abolition of Serfdom in Russia* (1954; now in its third edition) (both in Russian), in addition to a number of books on other nineteenth-century subjects. In the conclusion to his study of the reform, Zaionchkovskii discusses what is seen as its ambivalent contribution to the development of capitalism in Russia.*

P. A. Zaionchkovskii

Capitalism and the "Prussian Path" of Agrarian Development

A distinctive peculiarity of the Russian historical process was that the bourgeoisie did not play the role there which had been characteristic of it in the West during the period of the liquidation of feudalism and the consolidation of capitalism. In the West, the peasants had been liberated from the chains of feudalism by the bourgeoisie. In Russia, the bourgeoisie was incapable of leading the peasantry's revolutionary struggle for the abolition of feudal landownership. Consequently, the Russian bourgeoisie could not express the aspirations of the peasantry, which was striving for the complete liquidation of feudal relations.

It was the revolutionary democrats, whose ideology was formed in the 1840s, who stepped forward in Russia as the representatives of the enserfed peasants' interests. The revolutionary democrats advocated the complete liquidation of serfdom by means of a revolutionary overthrow of tsarism, which would have meant the development of capitalism unhampered by any survivals of the feudal-serf order.

A liberal ideology, bourgeois in content, took shape alongside the revolutionary-democratic ideology in that same period. The liberals were advocates of serf emancipation by reformist means, by means of an agreement with the government on the condition that *pomeshchik* landholding be preserved. The unrevolutionary character of the Russian bourgeoisie was conditioned by its political and economic dependence

*From P. A. Zaionchkovskii, *Otmena krepostnogo prava v Rossii (The Abolition of Serfdom in Russia)*. Second Edition, Moscow: Uchpedgiz, 1960, pp. 351–361. Footnotes omitted. Translated by Terence Emmons.

on tsarism. The experience of the political struggle in Western Europe, in the course of which the contradictions of capitalist society—between the bourgeoisie and its gravedigger, the proletariat—had already been revealed, was also of great significance in this regard. Throughout almost the entire nineteenth century, liberal ideology was represented by bourgeoisified gentry, a fact which left a definite imprint upon it. This was expressed alike in liberal projects for the solution of the peasant question and in the political demands of the Russian liberals, proposing, to one extent or another, preservation for the gentry of a leading role in the country's social life.

The revolutionary democrats and the liberals appeared as the advocates of two paths for the capitalist development of Russia. The former were advocates of a revolutionary path, signifying complete liquidation of the feudal-serf system and liquidation of *pomeshchik* landholding; the latter were advocates of a reformist path, signifying the development of capitalism under conditions by which feudal-serf survivals, whose foundation was the preservation of *pomeshchik* landholding, would continue to exist.

Although their class position gave them an interest in the liquidation of feudalism, the liberals, who represented the interests of the bourgeoisie, found themselves in one camp with the feudalists, and waged a struggle against them only over "the form and extent of concessions" . . .

The absence of a revolutionary class capable of leading the struggle of the peasantry—as either a bourgeoisie or a proletariat might have done—allowed the government to avert a revolutionary explosion and carry out the abolition of serfdom by means of a reform. The revolutionary situation of 1859–1861 did not grow into a revolution.

Despite its feudalistic character, the abolition of serfdom, called forth by the entire course of the country's economic development and instituted by tsarism out of fear of a revolutionary explosion, created the conditions for consolidation of the capitalist base. These conditions consisted of the personal emancipation of more than 20 million *pomeshchiks'* peasants who had been partially deprived of the means of production. Precisely as a result of the peasant reform and the subsequent process of capitalist development there was created an army of many millions of hired laborers, an army which had reached 10 million men by the early 1890s according to the data of V. I. Lenin. The personal emancipation of the peasants was one of the decisive factors assuring the victory of new relations of production. Transfer of the peasants to redemption (*i.e.*, their redemption of feudal rent) signified, essentially, the liquidation of feudal relations of production. Despite the preservation of survivals of the feudal-serf order in various forms of labor rent, capitalist relations of production gradually, if slowly, came to occupy a predominant position.

". . . The reform was the product of the development of a commodity economy," wrote V. I. Lenin, "and . . . its entire meaning and significance consisted of the fact that the shackles which had retarded and confined the development of that order were destroyed."

As a result of the abolition of serfdom, the capitalist form of property became dominant. But the 1861 reform did not fully destroy the foundation of the feudal mode of production—feudal ownership of land. As a result of the reform, the temporarily obligated relations, whose liquidation depended entirely on the will of the *pomeshchik*, were preserved for an indeterminate time. Thus, extraeconomic constraint was retained for a certain part of the peasantry, and those peasants who had concluded redemption agreements and had entered the category of so-called "proprietary peasants" also found themselves in complete dependence upon, and servitude to, the *pomeshchik* as a result of the rapacious character of the reform. All this constituted the preservation of survivals of the feudal-serf order, which found their main expression in the preservation of the labor-rent system. This, in its turn, called forth the development of capitalism in agriculture along the so-called "Prussian" path, characterized by the fact that, rather than being liquidated immediately, feudal-serf relations in agriculture were gradually adapted to capitalism, which preserved semifeudal features as a result.

Preservation of survivals of serfdom in the base determined in turn the viability of the old feudal political superstructure, which had made only a step toward adjustment to the new base.

The peasant reform, marking the first step in Russia's transformation into a capitalist state, also necessitated changes, in the spirit of bourgeois legality, in individual branches of the state edifice. However, the implementation of the bourgeois reforms occurred only under the influence of the situation of "social agitation and revolutionary onslaught" which forced the government to promulgate those reforms. Introduction of the *zemstvo*,[1] promulgation of the judicial reform which established the principles of bourgeois legal procedure, the new university statute, reform of the secondary schools, the urban statute of 1870, and, finally, the military reforms—all this characterized the evolution of the feudal order toward its transformation into a bourgeois monarchy. The implementation

of all these changes could not be consistent, because of the ambivalent nature of the bourgeois reforms. By means of isolated concessions, the government succeeded in preserving the autocratic-gentry character of the entire state system. The liberals rendered an important service in this. "The liberals," as Lenin noted, "wanted to 'free' Russia 'from above,' without disturbing either the monarchy of the tsar or the landholding and authority of the *pomeshchiks*, urging them only to make 'concessions' to the spirit of the times."

The institution of these reforms did not change the class character of the tsarist monarchy, which remained as before a dictatorship of the *pomeshchik* serf owners, while also enjoying a certain amount of support from the bourgeoisie. The preservation of tsarism as a feudal superstructure preserved the remnants of serfdom "which had outlived themselves long before and *could not have* survived one day longer without floggings, shootings, punitive expeditions, etc." [Lenin]. The interests of Russia's historical development demanded the liquidation of tsarism, which was the focal point of the remnants of serfdom.

The process of economic development in the postreform period was characterized by the consolidation and further growth of capitalism in all branches of the national economy. In agriculture, this process found expression in the differentiation of the peasantry; *i.e.*, in its gradual disintegration into a bourgeoisie and a proletariat; and also in the capitalist evolution of the *pomeshchik* economy. On the basis of a scrupulous study of statistical data, primarily from the *zemstvo*, V. I. Lenin in his work, *The Development of Capitalism in Russia*, ascertained the far-advanced process of peasant differentiation. Thus, according to the data from the late 1880s and early 1890s for twenty-one provinces, the number of farms without beasts of burden constituted 24.7

---

[1] The name given to the organs of limited self-government instituted in 1864, at both district and provincial levels.—Ed.

percent of the total; while farms with three or more head of beasts of burden comprised 20.7 percent. Despite the existence of the communal-equalizing principle of land allotment in the majority of provinces, actual land usage was far from equalized . . .

Capitalist production in industry developed at an even faster tempo. The culmination of the industrial revolution occurred in the postreform period, at about the end of the 1870s. Heavy industry began to develop with relative rapidity, having developed at an extremely poor rate in the prereform period. In the 1860s–1880s a new metallurgical region was developed in the Ukraine. Over the thirty-year period 1860–1890, the smelting of pig iron almost tripled—from 20.5 million to 56.6 million *puds*. In the Urals, however, the development of heavy industry proceeded slowly, as a result of the preservative of survivals of the feudal-serf order, and also as a result of the inability of the factory owners to adapt to the new capitalist economic methods.

A major influence on the development of the southern metallurgical region was exerted by the mining of iron ore in the Krivoi Rog region, beginning in the 1880s. The extraction of petroleum in the Caucasus, which had hardly existed before 1861, developed swiftly: While petroleum extraction had amounted to 557,000 *puds* in 1865, in 1890 it was 242,900,000 *puds*; and in 1895, 384,000,000 *puds*.

Significant growth in the production of the means of production was in turn creating conditions for the development of an internal market. Development of light industry, especially textiles, also proceeded rapidly. Production of cotton-weaving factories multiplied more than three times during this period. In monetary terms, the production of cotton factories increased four and one-half times during the thirty-year period from 1860 through 1890. Pro-

duction of means of production developed with significantly greater speed, however, than did production of means of consumption, a fact which created conditions for production on an expanded scale. General technical progress can be judged by the increase in steam-engine capacity. Thus, according to the data compiled by V. I. Lenin, between 1875 and 1892 the capacity of steam engines in European Russia (excluding Poland, the Caucasus, Siberia, and Turkestan) grew from 98,888 horsepower to 256,469 horsepower; *i.e.*, by more than two and one-half times; and for the entire empire, it grew from 114,977 to 345,209 horsepower.

The process of capitalist development was finding expression in a constantly growing concentration of production, which had attained a high level before the end of the nineteenth century: Nearly three-fourths (74.6 percent) of the total number of factory, mill, and metallurgical workers in European Russia were concentrated in enterprises with 100 or more workers; and nearly half of these were concentrated in enterprises with 500 or more workers.

The development of capitalism in both industry and agriculture and the social division of labor associated with this gave rise to a significant increase in internal trade, which in turn promoted the development of communications, both railroad and waterway: While in 1865 the total length of railways was 3,374 *verstas*[2], at the end of the 1890s the length of railroad lines was 36,611 *verstas*.

Thus, after the abolition of serfdom rapid capitalist development was occurring in all branches of the national economy as a result of the predominance of the new productive relations consolidated after the abolition of serfdom in 1861.

---

[2] One *versta* = 3,500 feet.—Ed.

The tempo of capitalist development could have been more rapid, however, if survivals of the feudal-serf order had not been preserved to a significant degree. These survivals retarded the economic development of the country and impeded the further development of the forces of production. Overproduction crises, resulting from the contradictions of a capitalist mode of production in combination with the preservation of feudal-serf relations, were longer and more protracted in character.

Survivals of the feudal-serf order were manifested above all in the preservation of *pomeshchik* landholding, on which in turn the political supremacy of the gentry rested. *Pomeshchik* landholding was the economic foundation for the remnants of serfdom. Preservation of *pomeshchik* landholding meant the development of capitalism along the so-called "Prussian" path, which was extremely agonizing for the peasantry. The peasantry labored under a double burden: that of feudalism and that of the survivals of serfdom. As a result of the rapacious character of the reform, the peasants fell into servitude under their former masters, acquitting under the guise of rent what was in fact the same old *barshchina*. The preservation of bondage and labor rent retarded in every possible way the development of capitalism in the village.

The existence of the labor-rent system of economy was conditioned not only by the preservation of *pomeshchik* landholding, but also, as Lenin noted, by the absence of the conditions necessary for the transition to capitalist production. One of the fundamental conditions for that transition was the possession by the estate owners of a certain quantity of monetary means, as required for the acquisition of agricultural implements and draft animals, and also for the hiring of a labor force. In addition, a

no less important condition for this was the organization of agriculture "... like any other commercial-industrial enterprise, and not like a seigneurial affair" [Lenin].

But despite the fact that the redemption operation gave the gentry a significant amount of the means required for reorganization of their economy, the means were not at hand, since the greater part of these sums went either to the liquidation of debts on the estates, or was spent unproductively. The Russian gentry, in addition, lacked the ability to transform their estates into commercial-industrial enterprises.

The preservation of survivals of the feudal-serf order in the village was also manifested in the existence of the commune, which had an exclusively fiscal-police character—in the political inequality of the peasants, etc. All this could not fail to exercise a definite influence on the general process of capitalist development in the country.

Analyzing the process of Russia's economic development after the abolition of serfdom, V. I. Lenin wrote: "If one compares the precapitalist epoch in Russia with the capitalist epoch . . . , it must be recognized that the development of the national economy under capitalism was extraordinarily rapid. If, however, one compares the actual speed of development with that which would have been possible, given the contemporary technological and cultural level as a whole, then it must in fact be recognized that the actual development of capitalism in Russia was slow. Nor could it fail to be slow, for in no capitalist country had traditional institutions, incompatible with capitalism and hindering its development, survived in such abundance . . ."

The situation of the peasants as a result of the preservation of *pomeshchik* landholding was extremely difficult. Lack of land, as a result of which the peasant found himself in bondage to the *pomeshchik;* the weight of redemption payments and other obligations; and, finally, a complete lack of rights—all this gave rise to degradation of the peasant economy and mass, systematic starvation of millions of direct producers. Accordingly, the peasant movement did not cease in the postreform period, but continued with periodic fluctuations in its proportions. In no way could the peasants accept the conditions in which they found themselves after having been robbed in 1861. In the prereform period the basic substance of the peasant movement had been the struggle for personal emancipation, which was inextricably bound up in the peasants' minds with the transfer to their ownership of at least that land which they had been cultivating. In the postreform period, the peasant movement acquired a predominantly agrarian character, consisting of a struggle for land, and first and foremost for the cut-offs.

The national peculiarity of the bourgeois revolution in Russia was its agrarian character. The fundamental problem of the revolution was the liquidation of *pomeshchik* landholding and of all the social and political survivals of serfdom. As V. I. Lenin wrote: "Eighteen sixty-one begat 1905."

Russia's entry into the epoch of imperialism, which was characterized by an extremely high degree of socialization of production, led to a sharp aggravation in the contradictions of capitalism, contradictions between the social character of production and the private-capitalist form of appropriation. The productive relations of capitalism no longer corresponded to the character of the new productive forces. This conflict between capitalist productive relations and the new productive forces acquired particular intensity in Russia as a result of the preservation of remnants of serfdom.

Following the abolition of serfdom, as in the prereform period, the bourgeoisie proved incapable of leading the struggle for the utilization of economic laws in the interests of society. Despite its subjective interest in the liquidation of the survivals of the feudal-serf order, the bourgeoisie could not carry this out because of its non-revolutionary character. Liquidation of the remnants of serfdom could be carried out only as a result of the overthrow of tsarism. The bourgeoisie, as represented by its liberal ideologues, was capable only of a "struggle" with the government in the form of turning to it with timid petitions contained in "most loyal" appeals. In the years immediately following the peasant reform only the peasantry, among all the contemporary social classes, was interested in a decisive elimination of the remnants of serfdom, by virtue of which the peasant movement objectively constituted a struggle for the final victory of the new relations of production.

The peasantry's struggle against the remnants of serfdom in the 1860s and 1870s was led by the ideologues of the peasantry—the revolutionary democrats, beginning with Chernyshevskii and ending with the revolutionary populists. . . . Irrespective of their subjective aspirations, the revolutionary populists fought for complete liquidation of the survivals of the feudal-serf order; *i.e.,* for the final victory of the new relations of production. However, revolutionary populism, with its essentially utopian theory of "peasant socialism," naturally could not lead the struggle of the popular masses against tsarism, the focal point of the remnants of serfdom.

As a result of the development of capitalism in the postreform period there arose a new social class—the proletariat—which took up the struggle against the capitalists. The proletariat was the only class capable of leading the struggle against tsarism. Indeed, it was only in league with the working class that the peasants succeeded in realizing their aspirations.

As a result of the Great October Socialist Revolution, carried out under the leadership of the Bolshevik party, the exploiting classes were overthrown and "in passing," "along the way," the tasks of the bourgeois-democratic revolution were accomplished: the remnants of serfdom were swept away.

One of the best books on Russian agrarian development between reform and revolution was published in England in 1930 by the émigré agricultural economist and former official of the Russian Ministry of Agriculture, G. P. PAVLOVSKY. His work was based on personal observations throughout the early twentieth century and extensive knowledge of the published sources. In this selection from his book, Pavlovsky disputes the widely held belief that it was the dimensions of their landholding and obligations which were primarily responsible for the plight of the peasants after 1861.*

G. P. Pavlovsky

Land Tenure, Technology, and the National Economy

The influence of the redemption payments ... was great and manifold. Not only did they increase the need for ready money among the peasantry generally, and thus contribute to the commercialization of peasant farming, but, in the case of certain large groups of peasants they proved a very heavy burden indeed. Since the valuation of the land transferred to the peasants was arrived at by the capitalization of the rent payable for its usufruct, and that rent depended primarily on the *obrok*, which the serfs in the district concerned used to pay before the Emancipation, in those localities in which the *obrok* used to be high, the payments, in spite of the relatively high rate of capitalization, were heavy. Moreover, while under serf-

dom, in the more agricultural provinces of Russia the majority of the peasants were kept on the *barshchina*, thus paying their dues in labour, and the *obrok* was mainly confined to those of them who, having some trade or other source of money income, could pay it more easily, now the system of money payments had been extended to the peasantry as a whole. The result was that, though, as compared with the *obrok*, the redemption payments were as a rule, rather lower, those peasants who used, before the Emancipation, to be on the *barshchina*, and could not easily reorganize their whole husbandry now, so as to get hold of the necessary cash, found themselves faced with a very difficult problem indeed.

*G. P. Pavlovsky, *Agricultural Russia on the Eve of Revolution.* London: George Routledge and Sons, Ltd., 1930; New York: Howard Fertig, Inc., 1969, pp. 78–88. Reprinted by permission. Footnotes omitted.

The position of the former State peasants, in this respect, as in others, was better than that of the former serfs. Unlike the latter, before the Emancipation, the State peasants, as a general rule, had all been on the *obrok,* and the latter, fixed under Count Kiselev on the basis of a general cadastre of State-owned land and moderate in amount, was left in force after the reform. When, in 1886, the redemption of their holdings was made compulsory, it served to fix the capital value of their holdings. Accordingly it was estimated that, on the average for European Russia, the amount of annual redemption payments per dessiatin in the case of State peasants was 0.83 roubles, while former serfs paid as much as 1.31 roubles: a difference of about 51%. According to the statistics of the Agricultural Commission of 1872 and of a Fiscal Commission of the same year, the total payments of the State peasants in thirty-seven provinces of European Russia (i.e. exclusive of the nine Western and South-Western provinces) amounted to 92.75% of the estimated net yield of their holdings, while those of the former serfs reached 198.25%. Both these comparisons, however, though true enough in so far as they show the advantages generally enjoyed by the State peasants, can hardly be accepted unreservedly. In the case of the first of them, it must be observed that the State peasants in their great bulk were concentrated in the remoter parts of the country, mostly outside the black-earth belt, and that, accordingly, their land being of less value, it was only natural that their redemption payments per dessiatin should be lower than those of the serfs, most numerous in the agricultural provinces of the black earth. The second comparison rests on the very unreliable basis of net yield, which is extremely difficult to ascertain statistically, and too

much importance should not, therefore, be attached to its actual figures. That the conclusions of the official and other inquiries, which pointed out the burdensome nature of the redemption payments, however, were substantially correct, was confirmed by the accumulation of large arrears in the installments, as well as by the generally precarious economic condition of the peasantry after the Emancipation. Whether the payments were absolutely too heavy, as numerous writers contend, and actually exceeded the utmost possible limits of the yield of the land under any conditions, it is hardly possible to decide, but, in any case, they proved too heavy for the great bulk of the peasants of nineteenth-century Russia, with her limited agricultural markets and her few facilities for the profitable disposal of either labour or produce. The fact was recognized by the Government, and by the Ukaze of December 28, 1881, the payments were reduced considerably. The reductions varied according to provinces, but for the whole country they reached 27% of the amount hitherto paid annually. From the eighties onwards, they could hardly be looked upon as a heavy burden, and, had the general economic development of the country in the second half of the last century been more rapid, they would not have exercised any real influence on the progress of the peasantry. That, in many cases, even after their reduction, the payments were still felt as a burden, only served to show that the commercialization of peasant farming, its transition from natural to money economy, had been proceeding very slowly indeed, and still left large areas and large groups of rural population practically unaffected by the influence of the market.

From what has been said above, one can see that, indeed, some of the causes of the "land-hunger" among certain groups of the peasantry, as well as of the impoverishment which was characteristic of the decades following the Emancipation, could be traced to the great reform. When, in 1861, the Russian peasant emerged from the long-drawn ordeal of serfdom, in some cases he suffered a reduction of his holding; and that reduction, whenever it had taken place, had certainly been responsible for the development of "land-hunger" among the groups concerned. In some cases, though there had been no reduction, the holdings were too small at the time of the Emancipation, and have not been increased in the course of the reform. According to Professor L. Khodskii, an eminent Russian economist and statistician, whose estimate is accepted by other authorities on the subject as the most reliable, the position of the peasantry in Russia, after the Emancipation, with regard to the sizes of holdings, was as follows. Taking as standards the average sizes of holdings of State and appanage peasants in every province, which he considered as sufficient for the full employment and support of a peasant family, he proceeded to the study of the grouping of peasants according to the sizes of their holdings, as compared with that standard. The results arrived at were that, of the State and appanage peasants, 50.7% had received holdings in excess of this norm; 35.6% had holdings of the average size, and 13.7% had holdings below the standards of sufficiency. In the case of serfs, the proportions respectively were 13.9%, 43.5% and 42.6%. Considering the peasantry as a whole, without making a distinction between the State peasants and the former serfs, and applying to it the results of the above computation, it will be found that the proportion of peasants with insufficient holdings in Russia, on the morrow of the Emancipation, could be put at about 30%. This percentage, though

certainly considerable, included all holdings below the standard of sufficiency, from the "gratuitous" plot of a dessiatin or so to anything just falling short of the fairly generous size of the average holdings of State and appanage peasants. All the rest—70% of the peasants—received holdings either sufficient or in excess of the norm. This calculation helps to reduce to measurable terms the extent of the influence exercised by the land-settlement of the peasants after the Emancipation on the origin and development of the agrarian problem, in so far at least as its most familiar aspect—the "land-hunger" of the rural population—is concerned. After the Emancipation, with 70% of the peasantry in possession of holdings either sufficient or more than sufficient, under existing conditions of cultivation and yield, to make them self-supporting, Russia could hardly be considered as having laid the foundation of the agrarian distress which had developed in the course of the following decades. Even among the rest, whose holdings were in a varying degree insufficient for their support, possibilities of economic progress were not entirely excluded. Indeed, even the minute size of "gratuitous holdings" had not always proved an insuperable obstacle on the way to prosperity, and in some cases, especially in the vicinity of large markets, their owners have made good by the development on them of vegetable gardening, fruit-growing or some other form of specialized production. In the case of families with relatively large, though still not self-supporting holdings, the problem could mostly be satisfactorily solved by the practice of some auxiliary occupation or casual employment in the neighbourhood of the village; sometimes by outside employment of some member or members of the family. In fact, all these means of eking-out an insufficient income from their land were largely practised in the greater part of the under-producing belt, with the result that, on the whole, the "land-hunger" and the agrarian crisis there, in spite of the poor quality of the soil, was less acute than in the black-earth zone. Yet, as a matter of fact, the agrarian distress involved ever-increasing masses of peasants all over the country, and especially in the more purely agricultural districts.

The development could be described, in general terms, as a rapid growth of rural population unaccompanied by a simultaneous progress in the yield of the agricultural industry and in the opportunities of employment of the excess of hands in the countryside. The forms assumed by the phenomenon, as well as the intensity of its manifestation, varied according to locality, but essentially it was the same everywhere, and was produced by a combination of causes. Of the latter, certain were rooted in the organization and conditions of the countryside and of farming, while others, and the most potent by far, had to be sought in the character and the evolution of the economic structure of nineteenth-century Russia.

Among the causes of agrarian overpopulation a prominent place must be given to the conditions of peasant tenure. It will be remembered that the bulk of the peasantry in Great Russia, as well as some of the peasants of White, Little and New Russia, held their land in common, subject to periodical or occasional redistributions of holdings among the members of the commune, under the system of communal tenure (*mir, mirskoie vladenie*). The alternative system, predominant in the Western, the South-Western and the Little-Russian or Ukrainian provinces, involved tenure in perpetuity (*podvornoie vladenie*). Under both systems the individual holdings of the peasants were scattered in open fields in more or less numerous strips. The number of strips varied greatly, according to the nature of the soil, the layout of the village land and the sizes of holdings. The principle was that, in every field, each peasant must have a share equal to that of any other. The cottages and farm buildings of the peasants were all built in the village, mostly in two rows facing each other on either side of a central street or main road. In the Northern provinces of Russia, where the soil is of very uneven quality and suitable land is relatively scarce, as well as in the agricultural centre, with its dense population and small holdings, the strips were often extremely narrow and very numerous. In the South and South-East, where the land in the steppes is more uniform, the number of strips was generally much smaller and they were wider, but here, owing to the often very large size of the villages, clustering round the sources of water supply or in other convenient places, this advantage was often counterbalanced by the important drawback of the remoteness of some of the land from the village and consequent difficulty of its proper cultivation. Here, some of the strips, lying miles away from the village, not only necessitated a great waste of time in reaching them and practically excluded all possibility of manuring in the usual way, but had to be left unattended, except for occasional visits, from sowing-time to the harvest. The mixing-up of strips, their often extremely small width and their remoteness from the village—features of open-field tenure familiar to the student of English farming before the enclosures of the eighteenth century—need no enlarging upon as obstacles to the progress of the agricultural industry. In Russia, by the most ardent opponents of the commune, the *mir* had often been saddled with the responsibility for these evils, which, however, in fairness, should be attributed not to it but to any form of open-field tenure.

Indeed, about the part played by the system of tenure in the development of the agrarian crisis in Russia much has been written. The village commune (*mir*), involving redistributions of land among its members, had been vigorously assailed by numerous opponents, ranging from Conservatives to Marxian Socialists, and no less vigorously defended by its partisans from the Slavophils and other sections of the Nationalist Right to the most advanced groups of the narodniki. Here, the *mir* must be taken for granted, and its influence on the development of the agrarian problem in Russia considered dispassionately from the economic standpoint. In the view of the present writer, the main count in the indictment against the *mir*, or redistributory rural commune, as such, was that it contributed to the development of agrarian overpopulation by relieving the individual peasant from responsibility for the excessive increase of his family. The task of finding room for any new member devolved on the commune, which did it at the expense of the whole village, at the cost of relatively small individual sacrifices. As to the rest, it may be said that, while it is perfectly true that communal tenure hinders agricultural progress by restricting individual initiative, this fault is not peculiar to the *mir*, but is shared by all forms of open fields, either in Russia, or in England before the enclosures and in Germany before the agrarian reforms of the nineteenth century. It must even be admitted that in a village commune with effective redistributions the evil of small scattered strips lends itself more easily to correction, while in open-field villages without redistributions it is unavoidably perpetuated and grows gradually worse. The special objection directed against the redistributory commune or *mir* that it hinders agricultural improvements by making the position of the peasant with regard to his land insecure, really applies only to capital improvements, which, however, it is hardly possible for any individual to undertake on his strips, either in the *mir* or, for that matter, in any open-field village with holdings in perpetuity. As to other improvements, such as the use of artificial fertilizers of improved implements and seeds, they can equally well be used under both systems, subject to the general limitations involved in open-field cultivation. The introduction of improved rotation encounters the same obstacles in both cases, compulsory cropping (*Flurzwang*, as it is called in Germany) being an unavoidable attribute of open fields. Moreover, open-field tenure, either under the communal system or in perpetuity, has that great drawback that, with it, the peasant farm, as an economic and technical entity, does not exist. The division of the peasant's holding, even if carried to extreme, does not involve the breaking-up of an efficiently constituted, well-balanced farm into a number of inconvenient fragments: a fact which effectively helps in eliminating all checks on the growth of rural population and contributes to the excessive subdivision of holdings and the consequent pauperization of the peasantry.

Thus, in the systems of tenure in general use among the peasants in Russia there were elements present which undoubtedly contributed, on the one hand, to the unreasonably rapid increase in the rural population and, on the other, to the slowness of agricultural progress. Besides, the sufficiency of the holding depends not only on its actual size, on the fertility of the soil and on the form of tenure. From the purely agricultural point of view, there is the constitution of the holding which has to be taken into consideration as an important factor. In other words, whether or not a holding of a certain size is sufficient for supporting its owner in reasonably comfortable conditions, depends on the harmonious combination in it of the various elements essential for its successful exploitation. Thus, especially under a three-course system of cropping, in which no grass crops are cultivated, besides a sufficient area of arable, there must be a corresponding area of meadows and pastures for the maintenance of a certain number of cattle. This was probably the weakest spot in the land-settlement of the peasants after the Emancipation, and with the increase in population and the extension of arable at the expense of grass, it has been growing worse ever since. In a large number of cases, sometimes throughout whole districts, it was not the sizes of the holdings, but the relative shortage in them of this essential element that was the root of the problem. Here, indeed, one could see the application of the "law of the minimum," as enunciated by Liebig with regard to the constitution and fertility of the soil, to the economic aspect of farming. On the average, under the three-course system, the area of meadows and pastures must be approximately equal to that of arable: a proportion of which, in most localities, the Russian peasantry fell very far short. By the close of the last century, the ratio, in the great majority of cases, did not exceed one-third or one-half of the arable. In the most densely populated agricultural provinces of Russia, there was only a fraction of a dessiatin of grassland for every dessiatin of arable: at its worst, in the province of Kursk that fraction did not exceed one-thirtieth. In the parts of Russia outside the black-earth, where land required heavy manuring, the extent of the available meadows was the principal factor in deciding on the area actually under plough. In most parts of the North and North-West of Russia, the abundance of forest pastures provided sufficient food for the live stock in the summer, but the feeding of cattle in the course of the long winter presented great difficulties. The position of the Russian peasant in this respect was very similar to that of the English open-field farmer of the period preceding the enclosures of the later seventeenth and the eighteenth centuries and the spread of grass and root crops. In the Northern half of the country, the shortage of meadows resulted, on the one hand, in the incomplete exploitation of the available arable: on the other, it did not permit to develop dairy farming or other branches of production based on live stock, without a radical change in the system of cropping, which would allow the introduction of grass in the rotation, but was extremely difficult under the existing system of tenure. In the black-earth belt, peasant farming was also crippled in the branches depending on live stock, and especially on cattle, while the land was being exhausted by the insufficiency or the complete absence of manuring. In all cases, the yield of peasant farming was reduced to below what it could have been, even under the prevalent systems of cropping and cultivation, had the constitution of holdings been well-balanced. The lack of balance, which, in many cases, was itself the result of the growth of rural population and the consequent extension of arable at the expense of grassland, in certain localities could be definitely traced to the conditions of the peasants' land-settlement on their Emancipation. This was the case particularly in the Northern half of Russia, where arable land was generally less valuable than meadows, which formed the principal source of the landowners' income and, moreover, required a minimum of labour for their exploitation. It was accordingly the grasslands that the landowners, in transferring part of their estates to their former serfs, were most anxious to keep. The reductions, therefore, in the sizes of peasant holdings at the Emancipation, which in some provinces of this region were very considerable, mostly involved grasslands. In the province of Novgorod, for instance, the total area of peasants' holdings was estimated to have been reduced at the Emancipation by roughly one-third (from 1,600,000 to 1,045,000 dessiatins), most of the difference being accounted for by meadows and pastures. The result of this was that, though the peasants' holdings in the province of Novgorod were among the largest in Russia, and averaged, in 1905, no less than 13.5 dessiatins per family, with only 4.8% of small holdings below 5 dessiatins, the peasantry was greatly handicapped by the difficulty of providing sufficient hay for the cattle in winter, and thus often prevented from making the best use of their land.

It would, indeed, be impossible even to attempt, in this brief outline of the origins and development of the agrarian problem in Russia, to enumerate and describe all the numerous factors which to a greater or lesser extent were responsible for the difficulties of the Russian countryside. The problem was exceedingly complex, and the important point was that, while, strictly speaking, the insufficient size of the holdings lay at its root for a considerable section of the peasantry, practically the whole of the rural population was involved in it in some way or other, irrespective of the area of land in their possession. In fact, whatever the sizes of holdings, the real trouble was that the land was not used to the best advantage, and that the yield of peasant farming was miserably low.

With the population increasing with great rapidity throughout the second half of the nineteenth century, two things were absolutely essential to prevent the development of an acute agrarian crisis. In the first instance, an outlet was needed for the growing surplus of rural population. Russia stood urgently in need of that exodus from the villages which, throughout Western Europe, with the development of capitalism, kept on depopulating the countryside and swelling the ranks of industrial workers at the expense of the peasantry. This exodus, helped by emigration to new regions on the confines of the Empire, was the only possible means for relieving the growing pressure of the population on the land and the rapid parcellation of holdings into units below the economic size. Then, secondly, in order to provide for the increased demand of the growing population for agricultural produce, the standards of cultivation had to be raised, and the yield of the land increased gradually. The two developments, as a matter of fact, depended to a large extent on each other, since the rural exodus due to industrial growth would have of itself provided the necessary stimuli for the improvement of cultivation by extending the market for agricultural produce. Here it is that the student of the Russian agrarian problem comes to face those general economic conditions of nineteenth-century Russia which, more than anything else, have been responsible for the agricultural and agrarian situation on the morrow of the Emancipation.

When, in 1861, Russia emerged from its old social and economic regime, essentially based on serfdom, she did so rather under the pressure of moral and political considerations, than because the change had been brought about by the course of her economic development, which had already evolved the necessary elements of a new system. Indeed, as a Great Power, Russia could not go on living on the meagre resources of a medieval economic organization and was urgently in need of substituting for that inadequate basis a modern economic system, able to bear the financial burdens of a great nineteenth-century State. Accordingly, the old system was done away with, but the new capitalistic organization, which would eventually put to profitable uses Russia's large natural wealth and make the country more prosperous and powerful than ever, had still to be evolved. This proved a laborious task, and the development of modern capitalism in Russia proceeded slowly. Starting practically without capital, which was still, in the main to be either accumulated or imported from abroad, it was only natural that Russia, in the course of the second half of the last century, should suffer from a surfeit of hands in the country, and that instead of rural exodus she should develop agrarian overpopulation. The increase in the volume of foreign and internal trade, which accompanied the construction of railways and the growth of steam shipping, had been the first to manifest itself, as a sign of new times. But it was not to trade that one had to look for an outlet for the surplus population of the countryside. Only a rapid growth of industry, organized on capitalistic lines on a large scale and giving employment to an increasing number of hands, could solve the problem satisfactorily. Industrial capitalism, combined with an extensive development of large, capitalistically-organized farming, would have provided remunerative employment both for the absolute surplus of rural population and for those peasant-farmers, who, being settled on insufficient holdings, were dependent on local earnings for their livelihood. Yet, until the close of the nineteenth century, neither industrial capitalism, nor large farming, had developed to a sufficient extent to relieve in any marked degree the pressure of population on the land. The accumulation of capital in a country still almost entirely agricultural proceeded slowly, while the sources of foreign capital available to Russia at the time had to be used almost exclusively for

the purpose of providing the country with at least a skeleton of the necessary network of railways. Moreover, during the first two or three decades after the Emancipation, which coincided with the reconstruction and industrial development of the United States after the Civil War, Russia had a powerful competitor on the foreign capital market. Neither did the conditions of the Russian currency before its stabilization and final reform in 1897 encourage investment there in preference to countries with stable exchange. Accordingly, though foreign capital was being invested in Russia to some extent, and more particularly in her railways, mining, textiles and metallurgical industries and oilfields, since the 'seventies, the scarcity has always been painfully felt. It may be said that, in the second half of the last century, industry and agriculture in Russia were locked together in a kind of vicious circle. The countryside stood in need of the rapid growth of industry as a market for its produce and an outlet for its growing surplus of hands. Without such outlets for its production of both foodstuffs and men, rural Russia, overcrowded and poor, could not aspire to prosperity. On the other hand, Russian industries, which were naturally confined to the home market for the disposal of their products, depended for their development on the progress of the peasantry and the gradual increase in their purchasing capacity. The combination of circumstances with which Russia had been faced after the Emancipation could not be described as favourable; in fact, the conditions were such, that progress in either respect was delayed. The vicious circle had to be broken through at some point, and this ... actually did take place at the close of the last and the beginning of the present century, when the forces of growth, hitherto stinted, were gradually released.

Suggestions for Additional Reading

The volume of Russian-language material on the serf emancipation is very large. The reader of Russian will find direction to the greater part of this literature through several bibliographies, including: V. I. Mezhov, *Krest'ianskii vopros v Rossii . . .* (St. Petersburg, 1865) and his *Zemskii i krest'ianskii voprosy . . .* (St. Petersburg, 1873), which together provide an exhaustive bibliography of literature on all aspects of the "peasant question" published up to the year 1871; and S. L. Avaliani, "Bibliograficheskii ukazatel' iubileinoi literatury o krepostnom prave i krest'ianskoi reforme 1861—19 fevralia—1911," in *Izvestiia Odesskogo bibliograficheskogo obshchestva,* 1911, vol I., part 3, which catalogues the enormous literature produced on the occasion of the reform's fiftieth anniversary. These specialized bibliographies, together with N. A. Rubakin, *Sredi knig,* vol. II (Moscow, 1913), and the bibliographical lists in A. A. Kornilov, *Kurs istorii Rossii XIX veka,* (2d ed. 3 vols. in 2; Moscow, 1918), provide access to the better part of the pre-Revolutionary literature on the reform. Soviet literature on the emancipation is reviewed and listed in two historiographical articles written at the 100th anniversary of the reform: B. G. Litvak, "Sovetskaia istoriografiia reformy 19 fevralia 1861 g.," in *Istoriia SSSR,* 1960, no. 6; and P. A. Zaionchkovskii, "Sovetskaia istoriografiia reformy 1861 g.," in *Voprosy istorii,* 1961, no. 2. *Istoriia SSSR. Ukazatel' sovetskoi literatury,* 1917-1952 gg. (2 vols. with supplements; Moscow, 1956-1958), is a general bibliography of Soviet work through 1952 on Russian history. Subsequent developments in Soviet historiography on the reform and the "peasant question," agrarian relations, etc., can be traced through the major historical journals, *Istoriia SSSR* and *Voprosy istorii,* and in the valuable serial editions published by the Soviet Academy of Sciences: *Ezhegodnik po agrarnoi istorii vostochnoi Evropy* and *Materialy po istorii sel'skogo khoziaistva i krest'ianstva SSSR.* Extensive bibliographies of works (primarily in Russian) on the history of the peasantry and agrarian relations from earliest times to the Revolution are provided in: G. T. Robinson, *Rural Russia under the Old Regime* (New York, 1932, and subsequent editions), and Jerome Blum, *Lord and Peasant in Russia from the Ninth to the Nineteenth Century* (Princeton, N.J., 1961).

Leaving the reader of Russian to these bibliographical devices, the following suggestions are restricted to works available in Western languages, and especially in English. A very useful but highly selective guide to works in English on modern Russian history is David Shapiro (compiler), *A Select Bibliography of Works in English on Russian History, 1801-1917* (Oxford, 1962).

There are in English a number of reliable survey histories of Russia from earliest times to the present. Among the best are: M. T. Florinsky, *Russia, A History and an Interpretation* (2 vols.; New York, 1961) and N. V. Riasanovsky, *A History of Russia* (New York, 1963). A stimulating unorthodox discussion of the span of Russian history is provided by B. H. Sumner, *A Short History of Russia* (New York, 1943, and other editions). An excellent survey of Russian history, written by prominent Russian émigré scholars, is Paul Miliukov *et al, Histoire de Russie* (3 vols.; Paris, 1932-1933), of which the first two volumes are now available in English translation (*History of Russia,* vols. I and II; New York, 1968). Valuable surveys of nineteenth-century Russia include: A. A. Kornilov, *Modern Russian History* (translated from Russian) (2 vols.; New York and London, 1916, and subsequent editions and abridgments); and the more recent S. Pushkarev, *The Emergence of*

Modern Russia, 1801-1917 (New York, 1963), and H. Seton-Watson, *Imperial Russia,* excerpted above.

Surveys of Russian social and economic history include: P. I. Lyashchenko, *History of the National Economy of Russia to the 1917 Revolution* (translated from Russian) (New York, 1949), a standard Soviet work and the only general survey of Russian economic history available in English; J. Mavor, *An Economic History of Russia* (New York, 1914; revised edition, 1925), a work whose title does not accurately mirror its contents but which does provide in English résumés of some classic Russian studies; D. S. Mirsky, *Russia: A Social History* (London, 1931); and B. Gille, *Histoire économique et sociale de la Russie* (Paris, 1949). Also worthwhile is B. Brutzkus, "The Historical Peculiarities of the Social and Economic Development of Russia," in R. Bendix and S. M. Lipset (eds.), *Class, Status and Power* (Chicago, 1953).

Taken together, J. Blum, *Lord and Peasant in Russia* and G. T. Robinson, *Rural Russia* provide a superior and remarkably coherent survey of the history of the Russian peasantry and agrarian relations from earliest times to the Revolution. The recently published collection of articles, W. S. Vucinich (ed.), *The Peasant in Nineteenth-Century Russia* (Stanford, Calif., 1968), provides a new look at various aspects of peasant life and culture, and several of its articles deal directly with problems related to the emancipation.

An excellent analysis of the structure and functioning of the landed estate in Russia before emancipation is M. Confino, *Domaines et seigneurs en Russie vers la fin du XVIIIe siècle* (Paris, 1963). The work also discusses changes in the agrarian economy before the reform and the development of abolitionist ideas in Russia. Two contemporary works which give much information about Russian society before 1861 and dwell in particular on gentry-serf relations are: Baron A. von Haxthausen, *Studien über die innern Zustände, das Volksleben und insbesondere die ländlichen Einrichtungen Russlands* (3 vols.; Hannover and Berlin, 1847-1852) (also available in a simultaneously published French edition and in an English abridgment); and N. Turgenev, *La Russie et les russes* (3 vols.; Paris, 1847). In addi-

tion to the works mentioned above and those excerpted in the first section of the present volume, the following studies relevant to the serf economy before 1861 may be mentioned: H. Rosovsky, "The Serf Entrepreneur in Russia," in *Explorations in Entrepreneurial History,* vol. 6 (May, 1954); L. Volin, "The Russian Peasant and Serfdom," in *Agricultural History,* vol. 17 (January, 1943); and M. Tugan-Baranovskii's classic *Geschichte der russischen Fabrik* (translated from Russian) (Berlin, 1900), which deals *inter alia* with many questions concerning peasant labor and the economic expectations surrounding the emancipation.

In addition to the works excerpted in the second section and the general studies mentioned (among which Kornilov, *Modern Russian History* deserves special mention in this regard), the preparation and implementation of the reform are discussed in the following works: T. Emmons, *The Russian Landed Gentry and the Peasant Emancipation of 1861* (Cambridge, Eng., 1968), which describes gentry involvement in the reform and the details of its preparation; R. Portal (ed.), *Le Statut des paysans libérés du servage, 1861-1961* (Paris and The Hague, 1962), a collection of articles and translations of documents concerning the preparation and execution of the reform; and W. E. Mosse, *Alexander II and the Modernization of Russia* (New York, 1958), a brief review of the "Epoch of Great Reforms" as a whole. See also S. Zenkovsky, "The Emancipation of the Serfs in Retrospect," *Russian Review,* vol. 14, no. 2 (1955).

A very considerable literature in Western languages is devoted to Russia's postemancipation agrarian development. In addition to the general works mentioned above and those excerpted in the text (among which the studies of Pavlovsky and Robinson deserve special attention), the following works may be noted as of interest: An expert analysis of the reform legislation in terms of its implications for future economic development, as well as a review of agrarian policies to 1914, is given in A. Gerschenkron, "Agrarian Policies and Industrialization, Russia, 1861-1914," *Cambridge Economic History of Europe,* vol. VI (New York, 1965). Valuable contemporary descriptions of Russian society in which much attention is paid to the postreform peasantry are: A. Leroy-Beaulieu, *L'Empire des tsars et les Russes* (3 vols.; Paris, 1889–1893) (translated into English as *Empire of the Tsars and the Russians* [3 vols.; New York and London, 1893–1896]); D. M. Wallace, *Russia* (2 vols.; London, 1877, and subsequent editions and abridgments); and Stepniak (S. Kravchinsky), *The Russian Peasantry: Their Agrarian Conditions, Social Life, and Religion* (New York, 1905). Several valuable contributions to the study of postreform rural Russia are contained in C. Black (ed.), *The Transformation of Russian Society: Aspects of Social Change Since 1861* (Cambridge, Mass., 1960). The debate between Populists and Marxists over the postreform development of Russia is discussed by A. P. Mendel, *Dilemmas of Progress in Tsarist Russia: Legal Marxism and Legal Populism* (Cambridge, Mass., 1961), and is directly represented in Western languages by Nicolas-On (N. Danielson), *Histoire du développement économique de la Russie depuis l'affranchissement des serfs* (Paris, 1902) and V. I. Lenin, *The Development of Capitalism in Russia* (Moscow, 1956), both translated from Russian. (Written in the

1890s, Lenin's work investigated the development of the internal market and the differentiation of the peasantry after 1861, and is the major source of the current Soviet interpretation of the results of the emancipation.) D. W. Treadgold, *The Great Siberian Migration: Government and Peasant in Resettlement from Emancipation to the First World War* (Princeton, N.J., 1957), discusses various aspects of the "peasant question" after 1861. See also: L. A. Owen, *The Russian Peasant Movement, 1906–1917* (London, 1937); J. Maynard, *The Russian Peasant and Other Studies* (London, 1942, and subsequent editions); P. Czap, "Peasant-Class Courts and Peasant Customary Justice in Russia, 1861–1912," *Journal of Social History*, vol. I, no. 2 (Winter, 1967); K. Kacharovksy, "The Russian Land Commune in History and Today," *Slavonic and East European Review*, vol. 7 (March, 1929); and B. Maklakov, "The Peasant Question and the Russian Revolution," *Slavonic and East European Review*, vol. 2 (December, 1923); ———, "The Agrarian Problem in Russia before the Revolution," *Russian Review*, vol. 9, no. 1 (1950).